The FLOW Series™ Presents

INTERVIEW INSIGHTS: A STRATEGIC APPROACH

Interview Insights: A Strategic Approach

Copyright © 2025 by The FLOW Series™

ISBN: 979-8-9927479-1-1

Dedication

For those figuring life out, here's to the courage it takes to start and the strength to keep going.

Contents

Foreword

Stepping into new opportunities, whether it's beginning your career, working through a transition, or exploring your next step, can feel overwhelming. There's no shortage of advice available, but sometimes what's needed most is the opportunity to pause, reflect, and gain perspective. That's why *Interview Insights: A Strategic Approach* was created.

At its core, Figuring Life Out from Within is the philosophy behind The FLOW Series™: a way of thinking that prioritizes understanding before action, reflection before reaction, and awareness before assumption. From that foundation, we focus on tools, perspectives, and approaches that support decisions grounded in who you are. Success isn't about fitting into a mold; it comes from understanding your strengths, recognizing your values, and choosing how you want to contribute.

This book is not only about interviews. It's about developing a sense of connection in conversations, recognizing the value you bring, and seeing that you have more influence over your career path than it may sometimes appear. You don't have to guess your way through this or carry the pressure alone. The insights here were built from challenges faced early in our own careers: the uncertainty, the pressure of proving yourself, the question of where to begin.

Wherever your path begins and wherever it leads, you belong in the spaces you're striving for. These pages are meant to offer the tools and insight to help you get there.

Thank you for allowing us to be a part of your story. We're excited to see where it takes you!

Sincerely,

The FLOW Series Team

Chapter One

The Interview Blueprint

"Success is where preparation and opportunity meet" –
Bobby Unser

1.1 Inside the Interview Process

Interviews are conducted in a variety of different formats, with each designed to assess specific qualities of a candidate's fit for the role. Whether it's assessing behavioral responses, technical proficiency, problem-solving capabilities, or cultural fit, each interview type serves a specific purpose in the hiring process. Understanding the nuances of these formats will allow you to show your adaptability, communication skills, and how you align with the potential employer's values and expectations. Effective preparation includes understanding these formats and customizing your methods to fit the specific requirements of each one.

Interview Styles and Their Focus

Behavioral Interviews: Behavioral interviews focus on how you've handled situations in the past to understand your potential for future roles. These questions ask you to think back on how you've navigated challenges in your work or at school.

- *What to Do*: Pull together examples that bring out your skills in leadership, teamwork, problem-solving, and adaptability. Focus on measurable outcomes, and connect each example directly to the role you're applying for, helping employers understand your potential impact.

- *Why It Matters*: Sharing specific examples of your past experiences gives interviewers a sense of your strengths and abilities. By providing these details, you help them see how your professional qualities align with what their team needs. When you describe how you've successfully applied your skills in previous roles, interviewers can better understand your potential fit and envision the contributions you'd bring to their organization.

Technical Interviews: Technical interviews test your skills and knowledge in areas like engineering, IT, and science. Interviewers are looking to see how you apply your expertise to real-world problems or tasks tied to the role.

- ***What to Do***: Start with the fundamentals: they give you a reliable way to evaluate challenges and apply proven methods. Then, build on that base: develop new skills through Udemy, sharpen your perspective with HBR webinars, and stay research-driven by reviewing current studies on Google Scholar. Using both the basics and the latest insights helps you approach problems with confidence, explain your ideas clearly, and show future employers or colleagues that you're serious about growing in your field.

- ***Why It Matters***: Succeeding in technical interviews strengthens your professional reputation and sets you apart in your field. It opens doors to roles at top companies, supports your career growth, and connects you with valuable industry contacts.

Case Interviews: Predominantly used in the consulting and finance sectors, case interviews challenge candidates to address and solve a business challenge, or analyze a case study, in real-time. This format tests analytical thinking, strategic decision-making, and practical application of business principles.

- *What to Do*: Familiarize yourself with common industry scenarios and practice breaking them down step by step. Use case studies to strengthen your ability to identify key issues, analyze patterns, and design responses that work in practice. Add resources from Mind-Tools to learn techniques for structuring problems, comparing options, and presenting your analysis so others can follow your reasoning and see the strength of your recommendations.

- *Why It Matters*: Case interviews mirror the type of challenges professionals face daily, requiring you to break down ambiguous problems, analyze data, and communicate solutions in a way others can act on. Preparing for them not only positions you to succeed in the interview but also builds the foundation for stronger decision-making and problem-solving throughout your career.

Interview Platforms

Panel Interviews: These interviews involve several interviewers at once, often from different parts of the organization. The format helps employers see how you communicate when multiple priorities and viewpoints are present.

- *What to Do*: Before the interview, review each panel member's role and background on LinkedIn. This gives you a sense of what they focus on and helps you prepare responses that reflect awareness of their responsibilities. During the conversation, share your attention across the group so each person feels involved. You might say something like, *"That point connects well with what you mentioned earlier,"* when a panel member builds on another's question. This keeps the discussion balanced and shows that you're listening to the group as a whole.

- *Why It Matters*: Performing well in a panel interview highlights your strong communication skills, active listening abilities, and composure in high-pressure situations. These qualities show that you can effectively join team environments, navigate interpersonal interactions, and engage with a wide range of stakeholders, making you a valuable asset in collaborative and cross-functional roles.

Virtual Interviews: Virtual interviews have become a vital part of the hiring process, offering flexibility and convenience for both candidates and employers. They allow you to connect with hiring teams from any location, breaking down barriers of geography and schedules. While the format is different, the opportunity to make a strong impression remains the same.

- *What to Do*: Test your internet connection, webcam, and microphone well before the interview so you can avoid last-minute issues. Get comfortable with the video platform: know how to join the meeting, adjust your settings, and use features like mute or screen sharing if they come up. Check your lighting and background to create a professional setting without distractions. Dress as you would for an in-person interview. Prepare a backup option, like the interviewer's phone number or email, which lets you take quick action and keep the conversation going even if technology gets in the way.

- *Why It Matters*: Virtual interviews reflect how well you prepare. When the technical setup is handled ahead of time, you can stay engaged in the discussion and show that you manage remote communication with the same consistency expected in any professional setting.

Purpose Behind Interviews

Employers use interviews to assess whether your experience, skills, and approach align with the role and the culture of the organization. At the same time, interviews give you the chance to demonstrate your professional strengths, share your enthusiasm, and show how you could contribute effectively to the team.

Remember that preparation should serve both sides. Use the conversation to learn about the position, the team, and the organization. Ask thoughtful questions so that by the end, both you and the employer can evaluate whether the opportunity is the right match.

1.2 Getting to Know the Company

Researching a prospective employer gives you insights that help you tailor your interview answers and express a real interest in joining their team. This preparation shows your proactive approach and dedication to understanding their organization. With this knowledge, you can explain how your skills and goals align with the company's mission, values, and current priorities.

The Importance of Preparation: Learning about the company's mission, culture, and objectives helps you respond to interview questions in a way that aligns with their values. You'll also be able to ask questions about how their growth can create opportunities for your own professional development, leading to a more balanced discussion.

- *What to Do:* Dedicate time to understand the company's mission, vision, and core values. Look into their latest projects, press releases, and any challenges they've faced recently. This view allows you to see where the role you're applying for fits within the larger picture of the company's objectives. Based on your research, develop questions that reflect your knowledge of the company's current state and your interest in its future. These questions could relate to recent awards or acknowledgements, ongoing projects, or how the role contributes to strategic goals.

- *Why It Matters*: Familiarizing yourself with the company's mission, culture, and goals helps you align your responses with their vision. This knowledge also gives you the chance to ask about how the company's direction can support your professional growth, creating a more engaging discussion. Understanding this connection allows you to highlight where your goals intersect with theirs, emphasizing the impact you could make.

Sources for Research: Researching a potential employer gives you the background needed to understand their history, culture, and industry position. Take a strategic approach by consulting various reliable sources to gain a well-rounded view of the organization. This broad perspective allows you to connect more effectively with the team and align your skills with their needs.

- *What to Do*: Begin your research with the company's official website to learn about its mission, values, and latest projects. Follow the company on social media to stay updated on recent news and the tone of their public interactions. For help reviewing your own professional presence online, see Toolkit 5: Digital Footprint Workshop. For insights into the company's market position and industry challenges, checkout accessible resources like Google News for current events, LinkedIn for industry-related posts and discussions, and Google searches for recent analyses on the sector.

- *Why It Matters*: Taking time to understand the company shows you're prepared to contribute, not just explore options. It demonstrates initiative, reinforces your interest in their mission, and gives you the insight to identify where you add value while also deciding if the team's direction fits your own goals.

1.3 Developing Your Professional Narrative

Defining Your Unique Value: Identifying what sets you apart means considering more than your skills and job history. Think about key achievements, the challenges you've overcome, and the perspectives you bring. Think about the feedback you've gathered from team members, performance assessments, and any formal recognitions. This self-assessment builds confidence and lets you communicate what makes you a unique addition to any team.

- *What to Do*: To recognize what sets you apart, review your experiences from work, volunteering, school, or personal projects where your efforts led to a clear result. Look for achievements that show initiative, skill, or impact: these are the stories that highlight why you bring value in ways others may not.

- *Why It Matters*: Understanding your strengths changes how you communicate with employers. Instead of listing tasks, you can explain how your skills solve problems the role demands and share examples of where you've done it before. This makes your application more persuasive and shows employers the specific contributions you're prepared to bring to their team.

Building Your Personal Story: Your personal story is your opportunity to connect your experiences directly to the role. A clear story shows interviewers how you think, what motivates you, and why your skills fit their needs.

- *What to Do*: Think about situations from school, internships, or past jobs where you used strengths such as leadership, collaboration, or innovation. Focus on times where you solved problems, made decisions, or achieved results that had a direct impact. For example, you might describe guiding a group to meet a goal, resolving an issue under pressure, or suggesting an idea that improved the outcome. Use the STAR method to structure your story: describe the situation, explain the task, outline your actions, and highlight the result. For a more detailed overview of STAR, refer is section 2.3 in Chapter 2 of this book. Choose examples that connect directly to the requirements of the role, and practice telling your story out loud until it feels natural.

- *Why It Matters*: Employers look for candidates who can connect past experiences to future responsibilities. A well-structured story shows that you understand your strengths, know how to apply them, and are prepared to bring that value to their team.

Recognizing your strengths is the starting point; the real value comes from learning how to translate them into strategic stories. In the sections ahead, we'll continue building on this foundation as we look at additional ways to prepare, before turning to how these stories show not just what you've done, but the judgment and reasoning behind your actions. This approach creates the kind of insight that makes employers pay closer attention.

1.4 The Confident Edge

How you approach an interview starts with your mindset. Taking a moment to prepare mentally can make all the difference; it helps you stay calm under pressure, think on your feet, and engage naturally throughout the conversation. Remind yourself of the value you bring and the effort you've invested in getting ready. Confidence sets the tone for how you come across from the moment the interview begins, and interviewers notice the calm in your voice, the logic in your answers, and your ability to stay composed throughout the conversation.

Mindset and Attitude: Your attitude often speaks before you do; preparation influences how interviewers interpret your explanations and the strength they see in your reasoning. Instead of viewing the interview as a test you need to pass, think of it as a conversation to learn whether you and the role are the right match. When you trust your abilities and know the value you bring, interviewers notice it in the way you speak, carry yourself, and connect with them.

- *What To Do*: Take a few minutes each day to reflect on your accomplishments and how they prepare you for this opportunity. Write down specific skills, experiences, or moments you're proud of, and use this list as a reference point while preparing for the interview. Practicing statements such as, *"I have the skills and experience this role requires,"* or *"This is my chance to show what I can do, and I'm ready,"* helps you internalize your strengths so they're easier to communicate during the interview. For structured prompts that help you take a closer look at your progress, see Toolkit 4: Post-Interview Analysis Template.

- *Why It Matters*: How you think about yourself influences the way you connect with others. This self-assurance allows you to highlight your strengths and stay focused during the interview. Preparation is the foundation of confidence: practice your pitch and review your achievements so you can explain them clearly to employers during the interview.

Stress Management Techniques: Interview anxiety is common, but it doesn't have to determine how you perform. Stress can make it harder to think clearly, which can hold you back from showing the full range of your abilities. Practicing simple stress management techniques helps you slow your pace, collect your thoughts, and explain your experiences in a structured way.

- *What To Do*: Interviews can feel overwhelming, but preparation reduces uncertainty, which is often the biggest source of stress. Review your resume, practice sample interview questions, and research the company so the basics feel familiar. Build in short resets for yourself: controlled breathing to slow your pace, light stretching or a walk to release tension, and visualization exercises to strengthen a positive mindset. Remind yourself that preparation gives you the knowledge to answer questions, while stress management determines how effectively that knowledge is delivered.

- *Why It Matters*: Unmanaged stress can pull your attention inward, toward self-criticism or second-guessing, rather than keeping you engaged with the interviewer. Stress management helps you redirect focus to the conversation itself, which is where the real connection is built. This presence not only improves how you respond but also how you are perceived.

Visualization for Success: Taking a few minutes to picture yourself succeeding in the interview allows you to practice success before you step into the room. By rehearsing the experience in your mind, you create familiarity with the setting and strengthen your ability to stay composed during the actual interview.

- *What To Do*: Set aside time to mentally walk through each stage of the interview. Picture yourself entering the room with an upright posture, making eye contact, and offering a confident greeting. Imagine taking your seat with both feet on the floor and hands resting naturally. See yourself listening without interrupting, pausing briefly before answering, and structuring your responses around one main idea at a time. Visualize the interviewer nodding or taking notes as you speak. Conclude by rehearsing a closing statement that thanks them for their time and reinforces your interest in the role before you exit.

- *Why It Matters*: Visualization strengthens the link between thought and action. By mentally practicing the interview, you reduce hesitation, improve recall of specific examples, and keep a steady pace in your answers. This preparation ensures that what you intend to communicate is reflected clearly in both your words and your presence.

1.5 Interview Success Framework

Mock Interviews: Mock interviews let you practice in conditions that resemble the real conversation. They help you rehearse your delivery, receive direct feedback, and understand how your responses come across to an employer.

- *What To Do*: Identify the most common questions in your field and role. If you're in marketing, for example, prepare for questions such as, *"How would you handle a campaign with limited resources?"* or *"Describe a time you used data to improve results."* Ask a mentor, colleague, or friend to play the interviewer and provide candid feedback. Record the session or rehearse in front of a mirror to check your pacing, tone, and body language. Refine your timing to show control over your delivery. This reinforces your ability to prioritize key points, avoid digression, and adapt your level of detail to the interviewer's needs.

- *Why It Matters*: Mock interviews give you data about your performance that preparation alone can't provide. They expose gaps in your reasoning, highlight the strength of your examples, and show whether your delivery aligns with the impression you want to create. This feedback loop strengthens both the substance of your answers and the consistency of your presentation.

Professional Presentation: First impressions in an interview often come from how you present yourself before you speak. Dressing in line with the company's culture and carrying yourself with confident demeanor sets a professional tone from the start.

- *What To Do*: Pay close attention to your posture and gestures during everyday interactions to become more aware of your nonverbal cues. Practice offering a firm handshake and a natural smile in casual settings so they feel authentic in the interview. Use group meetings, video calls, or networking events as practice grounds to refine how you sit, stand, and engage with others. These habits strengthen your ability to project consistency between how you see yourself and how others perceive you.

- *Why It Matters*: Your body language influences how interviewers interpret your answers. Upright posture signals attentiveness, direct eye contact shows you're engaged with the conversation, and a measured tone communicates control. These habits build consistency, allowing you to present yourself professionally without it feeling rehearsed.

Logistics and Timing: A little extra planning can make your interview day less stressful. Whether in-person or virtual, controlling these details in advance reduces uncertainty and allows you to focus on the discussion once the interview begins.

- *What To Do*: Double-check the interview date, time, and format, and place them in your calendar with reminders. If meeting in person, confirm the address, review directions, and allow extra travel time in case of delays. Identify an alternate route as a safeguard. For virtual interviews, test your video platform well before the meeting. Check your camera, microphone, and internet connection, and ensure your background is neat and distraction-free. Lay out items such as your resume, notes, or supporting documents so they are within reach.

- *Why It Matters*: When the logistical details are under control, you can focus entirely on the conversation and your strengths. Being on time and prepared shows respect for the interviewer's time and creates a positive first impression. Managing these details also helps reduce stress, so you can approach the interview with a clear head. A smooth start sets the tone for the entire meeting, allowing you to connect with the interviewer and present your qualifications without unnecessary distractions.

1.6 Key Takeaways: The Interview Blueprint

This chapter analyzed the main interview formats and connected each to strategies that improve performance. We showed how preparation helps you deliver structured responses, how learning about company culture guides the tone and examples you choose, and how professional presentation affects whether you are viewed as able to handle responsibilities without close oversight. What follows is a recap of the key points designed to help you apply these strategies directly in your interview preparation.

Key Takeaways

Section 1.1: Inside the Interview Process

- *Understand Interview Types and Expectations*: Each interview type, whether behavioral, technical, or case-based, has its own focus. Understanding these formats allows you to customize your responses to focus on your strengths and align with what the employer is looking for.

- *Show You're Up for the Challenge*: Not every interview follows a script. When a question takes an unexpected turn, explain how you focused on the main point, organized your response, and connected it back to the role. Interviewers take away more from how you worked through the challenge than from the specific details of your response.

- *Make Your First Impression Count*: Interviews quickly establish how employers assess potential. Early in the conversation, when discussing your experience, describe a situation where you adjusted your approach and produced a clear outcome. Interviewers listen for how you define the issue, explain your reasoning, and account for the outcome, because those elements align directly with how the role is performed.

Section 1.2: Getting to Know the Company

- *Speak Their Language*: When you understand what the company values, you can frame your answers in a way that reflects those priorities. Doing so shows that you've taken the time to learn how the organization defines success and that you can position your contributions in alignment with their goals.

- *Express Commitment to Growth*: Coming prepared with insightful questions shows that you're invested in the company's direction and see yourself as part of its progress. This approach communicates that you're ready to contribute to future goals rather than simply take a role as it exists today.

Section 1.3: Developing Your Professional Narrative

- *Bringing Your Unique Strengths to the Forefront*: Identifying what sets you apart extends further than listing skills on a resume. It involves incorporating achievements you've delivered, challenges you've overcome, and perspectives you've developed through experience. Presenting your strengths through real outcomes helps interviewers understand how you've made decisions and delivered results in situations similar to theirs.

- *Connecting Your Past to Your Future*: Frame your story so it ties your past achievements to the organization's present needs. This approach shows that you can contribute from the start while also evolving alongside the role and the company.

- *The Power of Self-Awareness*: Understanding your personal story allows you to identify patterns in how you've grown, the strengths you rely on most, and the lessons that shape your approach to work. Sharing this perspective shows that your development is intentional and that you know how to apply past learning to future challenges.

Section 1.4: The Confident Edge

- *Confidence Starts in Your Mind*: Think of mindset as the filter through which every interaction in the interview is expressed. It determines not only what you say, but how effectively you say it, influencing both your answers and the rapport you build.

- *Stay Calm, Stay Confident*: Anxiety before an interview is expected; the distinction lies in whether it unsettles you or strengthens you. Managing stress allows you to maintain composure, which influences not only how you answer but also how your presence is perceived throughout the conversation.

- *Visualize Your Success*: Taking time to imagine yourself in the interview helps you anticipate the flow of the conversation and the presence you want to bring. This practice reduces uncertainty, allowing you to remain composed and adjust to the natural flow of the dialogue.

Section 1.5: Interview Success Framework

- *Practice Makes Prepared*: Engaging in mock interviews gives you a chance to test not only your answers but your thought process. Incorporating targeted questions with constructive feedback helps you identify blind spots, refine how you explain complex ideas, then carry that discipline into real interviews.

- *First Impressions Matter*: Initial judgments are made quickly, often before you speak. Understanding the environment you are entering and presenting yourself in ways that align with it shows awareness, making it easier for others to focus on the substance of what you bring to the discussion.

Every interview is more than a test of knowledge; it's an opportunity to show how your experiences, values, and goals connect with what an employer needs. Preparing with this in mind shifts practice from memorizing answers to refining how you interpret questions, organize your thoughts, and connect them to what matters in the role. Remember, the process is as much about how you evaluate opportunities as it is about how employers evaluate you.

"The best way to predict the future is to create it." – Peter Drucker

Chapter Two

Your Story, Your Strength

"There is no greater agony than bearing an untold story inside you." – Maya Angelou

2.1 Telling Your Story

Focus on stories from your personal, academic, and professional life that demonstrate resilience, creativity, and adaptability. Choose real examples that show how your background connects with the employer's values and highlight your ability to communicate effectively and build connections with others.

Elements of a Good Narrative: When you're in an interview, a strong narrative can set you apart. Let's break down the key pieces that make your story memorable:

- *Context*: Lay the groundwork by explaining the situation, your role, and the responsibilities involved. This gives the interviewer the background they need to understand the circumstances and recognize the value of what you accomplished.

- *Challenge*: Describe a situation where you faced a tough situation. Share how it connected to your responsibilities and why the situation required your attention. This gives the interviewer a clear sense of the issues you had to address and the impact you made.

- *Action*: Outline the steps you took to overcome the challenge, focusing on your problem-solving and creative approach. This is a great way to show the interviewer how you handle conflicts and maintain your composure under pressure.

- *Result*: End your story by focusing on the results of your efforts. Whether it was a success or a learning opportunity, this is where you call attention to your contributions and the lessons that shaped your growth. Think about what you learned from the experience and how it prepared you for future roles. For help preparing these examples so they're organized and interview-ready, see Toolkit 1: Personal Pitch Workshop.

2.2 Capturing Your Best Moments

Inventory of Experiences: Think about the projects you've worked on, the challenges you've faced, and the successes you've enjoyed. These moments highlight the skills you've built, the strengths you bring to the table, and the qualities that make you stand out as a candidate.

- *Achievements*: Look back at the times in your life that really stand out. What did you achieve, and how did you make it happen? Write down those successes, focusing on the skills and strategies you used. When you can, include numbers or concrete results to add weight to your story and show the specific impact of your contributions.

- *Challenges Overcome*: We've all had those moments where things get really hard. What are some challenges you've overcome? Write down how you faced those situations, the steps you took, and how you stayed strong in situations that tested you the most.

- *Teamwork*: Reflect on times when collaboration shaped the outcome. Focus on your role, what the group reached together, and how this shows your ability to contribute within diverse teams to deliver shared goals.

- *Leadership and Problem-Solving*: Reflect on moments where you took the lead on a group project or faced a challenging situation at work. Describe how you handled it, the choices you made, and how your approach contributed to the outcome.

Selecting the Right Stories: When it comes to sharing your experiences, choosing the right stories is just as important as the stories themselves. Each example you share should serve a purpose: showing your fit for the role or the strengths that set you apart.

- *Matching Job Description*: Select stories that highlight the specific skills and qualities directly relevant to the job. Consider what the employer values most, and use examples that connect your past achievements directly to the requirements of the role.

- *Reflecting Company Values*: Share stories that echo the company's core values and mission. This is also a great opportunity to show how your unique perspective can support both their goals and long-term vision.

- *Diversity of Experiences*: Reflect on the variety of roles and challenges you've faced. Each one adds to your story and shows your ability to adapt and thrive in different situations.

- *Outcome Focus*: Share stories of how your actions led to positive outcomes, using specific data or examples. This makes it easier for interviewers to see the real impact you've had and the value you can bring.

2.3 Structuring Your Stories with STAR

Introduction to the STAR Method

Imagine this scenario: you're in an interview, and it's time to talk about your experiences. How do you share your story in a way that engages the interviewer and shows the value you bring? That's where the STAR method comes in. Think of it as a guide to structure your answers. You start by setting the scene (Situation), then explain what needed to be done (Task). Next, you describe what you did (Action), and finally, you close with the outcome (Result). This approach ensures you show how you've handled challenges and the impact of your contributions.

Applying STAR to Your Stories: To apply the STAR method to your stories, follow these step-by-step instructions:

- *Situation*: Picture yourself sharing your story with a colleague over coffee. Start by giving them a snapshot of the situation, just enough to make it interesting. If you were leading a project, describe the goal and the early challenges you faced.

- *Task*: Next, focus on what you needed to accomplish and why it was important. This is your chance to show the specific role you played in driving progress. Whether you were improving a process, solving a problem for others, or working toward a challenging target, explain what drove you and the impact of your contribution.

- *Action*: Let's shift our attention to how you addressed the challenge. What steps did you take, and how did you approach the problem? Think about your contributions, whether it was thinking outside the box, collaborating with others, or sheer determination; and highlight how your efforts strengthened the team's success.

- *Result*: Now, let's talk about the difference you made and use concrete results to tell your story. Instead of just stating that the project was successful, show the specific results you delivered with measurable outcomes, like a 20% efficiency increase and meeting your personal goal to enhance your communication skills with stakeholders. Think about what you learned from the experience and how it shaped both your professional approach and personal development.

2.4 Shaping Your Story for Any Audience

Having a set of go-to stories is great, but interviews often call for the ability to adjust these stories to align with the different ways interviewers frame their questions. Here's how you can make your storytelling more flexible:

- *Understand Your Story's Core*: Get to the heart of your stories. Focus on the challenges you faced, the actions you took, and the results you achieved. When you understand these core elements, you can tweak your story to fit different questions while still emphasizing the value you brought.

- *Practice Different Scenarios*: Prepare stories that cover a broad range of skills and outcomes. This way, you can easily adapt your responses to fit questions about leadership, teamwork, innovation, or bouncing back from setbacks. The more scenarios you practice, the more natural it becomes to adjust your answers in the moment without losing focus or confidence.

- *Hear, Reflect, Respond*: Imagine the interview as a conversation with a mentor. Share your experiences in a way that feels natural, focusing on the skills the employer values most. Listen carefully to the question, take a brief moment to reflect, and then respond with an example that shows how your abilities connect directly to what the role requires.

- *Learn from Experience*: Walk through the actions you took and what you learned along the way. Share how these situations prepared you for what comes next, focusing on how you learned from them and your talent for finding value in every experience. When you show that you can reflect and grow, interviewers see not just what you've done, but how you'll continue to contribute in the future.

2.5 Refining How You Respond

The STAR method is a great starting point for creating your interview responses. But to really stand out, add personal insights, emotions, and reflections to your stories. This not only helps you share information but also creates a stronger connection with your interviewer.

Think of it this way: when you share what happened, how you felt, what you learned, and how it strengthened your perspective, you give the interviewer a true sense of who you are. Those details bring your stories to life, leaving an impression that lasts well beyond the interview.

Bringing Your Stories to Life: The more engaging your stories, the more they'll connect with your interviewer. Try these tips:

- *Share Your Thought Process*: Take interviewers inside your mind as you recount your experiences. What were you thinking? How did these moments strengthen the way you approach future challenges? By sharing these insights, you highlight your problem-solving skills and your ongoing commitment to professional growth.

- *Share the Heart Behind Your Story*: Describe the emotions you felt during key moments. Whether it was excitement, satisfaction, or pride, these emotions bring your stories to life and make them more relatable, helping interviewers connect with the person behind the achievements.

- *Show How You've Evolved*: Wrap up your stories by highlighting the lessons you've learned and how these experiences have strengthened your development. It's a great way to show interviewers that you're continually adapting and ready to apply past insights to drive your future success. If you'd like a structured way to review your experiences and what they show about your approach, see Toolkit 4: Post-Interview Analysis Template.

Addressing Failure and Growth: Talking about challenges can emphasize your strengths when you frame them in a positive light. Here's the best way to share these moments:

- *Flip the Script on Challenges*: When setbacks come up, frame them as sources of insight by explaining what you learned, how you adjusted, and how those lessons shape the way you approach new situations. Interviewers value this reflective capacity because it shows that you don't just recover from setbacks; you refine the way you analyze problems and strengthen how you respond in the future.

- *Use Lessons to Guide Future Choices*: Think about the situations that demanded the most of you and the perspective they gave you. Share how those insights now shape your decision-making and interactions at work, showing growth in the way you operate today.

- *Prove Your Ability to Adapt*: When describing challenging experiences, emphasize the choices you made: how you identified options, applied new approaches, or developed skills in response. Doing so highlights adaptability as problem-solving in action, showing interviewers that you can bring the same resourcefulness to their environment.

2.6 The Power of Practice

Elevate Your Storytelling: Storytelling is how you translate personal experiences into professional relevance. Through practice, you learn to present situations in a way that highlights the context you faced, the reasoning behind your choices, and the results that followed without overwhelming your audience. To strengthen your storytelling:

- *Rehearse and Refine*: Rehearsing your stories out loud helps you recognize whether the meaning you intend is the meaning that comes through. With each rehearsal you make small adjustments: balancing pacing, adding depth where needed, so your delivery aligns more closely with the purpose behind your story.

- *Record and Review*: Hearing yourself played back offers distance from your performance. It allows you to notice habits you might overlook in real time and to adjust how your message comes across, from the strength of your voice to the balance of detail in your story.

- *Get a Fresh Perspective*: Inviting feedback from people you trust adds another layer to your preparation. Their input highlights where your delivery already reflects your intent: where small adjustments in detail, tone, or pacing can sharpen the impact of your story. When you reach out for perspective, see Toolkit 3: Feedback Request Template for ways to frame questions that draw out specific insight.

- *Utilize Online Tools*: Digital interview platforms such as Huru.a i and Google's Interview Warmup simulate the unpredictability of real conversations in a controlled space. Their automated feedback allows you to isolate specific aspects: timing, word choice, and delivery, refining them with each attempt and turning practice into an iterative process of improvement.

Simulated Success: Practicing through mock interviews shows the recurring patterns behind behavioral questions. In a practice setting, you learn to connect your stories to the qualities interviewers are evaluating; problem-solving, adaptability, and growth help you present examples that speak directly to what the role expects.

- *Connect with Peers and Mentors*: Peers and mentors bring different perspectives to your preparation. Peers help you hear how your stories sound to someone at your level, while mentors provide context from experience, creating a dual lens that shows how you come across in the moment and how your responses reflect longer-term growth.

- *Feedback Loop*: Use mock interviews to bring to light what you can't see on your own. Feedback exposes blind spots in both content and delivery, giving you the chance to refine your stories so they communicate the reasoning behind your choices, not just the high-level details.

2.7 From Insight to Action

What often distinguishes candidates in interviews is not the stories they bring in, but how they use them. Listening carefully to each question allows you to judge which example is most relevant to the discussion and to adjust when the conversation shifts. This adaptability shows that you can recognize when a question is asking for evidence of leadership, problem-solving, or collaboration, and select a story that makes that capability clear.

Adapting to Various Interview Formats: The format of an interview can shape how you share your story. Here are some tips to help you adjust your approach for different formats:

- *Virtual Interviews*: Without face-to-face interaction, interviewers focus on how you sound. Speaking at a measured pace and pausing for emphasis makes your responses easier to process and ensures your points come through as intended.

- *Panel Interviews*: When answering in a panel interview, start by focusing on the person who asked but bring the entire group into the response. This approach demonstrates awareness, inclusivity, and the ability to communicate in a way that keeps everyone engaged in the discussion.

- *Informal Interviews*: Informal conversations often give interviewers a closer look at your interpersonal style. They reveal how you listen, how you engage in conversation, and whether you can share relevant insights in a way that fits the flow of the discussion.

2.8 Key Takeaways: Your Story, Your Strength

As we wrap up this chapter, remember that well developed stories provide the foundation; the delivery gives it impact. Storytelling becomes the point where planning is translated into performance, expressing not only past outcomes but the ability to contribute in real time. Each example shared reflects judgment, adaptability, and communication; interviewers use these factors to understand how a candidate thinks through challenges and applies past lessons to new situations.

Key Takeaways

Section 2.1: Telling Your Story

- *Your Story Matters*: Each personal, academic, and professional experience adds to a narrative; it shows how problems have been approached, lessons applied, and results achieved. When these stories are framed to reflect employer needs, they provide direct evidence of judgment, adaptability, and the capacity to collaborate effectively across different situations.

- *The Power of a Good Narrative*: A well-structured story does more than describe events; it shows reasoning. By moving from context to challenge, through action and into results, candidates show how they assess situations, prioritize choices, and use past outcomes to inform present opportunities.

- *Bringing Your Story to Life*: A refined story allows interviewers to follow how a challenge was defined, why certain actions were prioritized, and how the outcome was interpreted. This gives them evidence of reasoning that extends beyond the event itself into how a candidate is likely to approach future work.

Section 2.2: Capturing Your Best Moments

- *Inventory of Experiences*: Across achievements, challenges, and collaborative efforts, what sets a story apart is its impact. When outcomes are linked to specific actions, interviewers gain a clear picture of contribution rather than activity.

- *Selecting the Right Stories*: Not every experience carries equal weight. Choosing those that align with the role and reflect organizational values ensures interviewers see the connection between prior contribution and the responsibilities ahead.

Section 2.3: Structuring Your Stories with STAR

- *Applying STAR to Your Stories*: The STAR method provides a disciplined framework for responses: situation, task, action, result. Organizing experiences this way ensures that interviewers can follow context, see how decisions were made, and evaluate the impact of the outcome.

Section 2.4: Shaping Your Story for Any Audience

- *Aligning Your Story with the Listener's:* Stories that focus on details tied to interviewer goals create a clear connection between past actions and present expectations; this focus clarifies how past contributions fit within the scope of what the position requires.

Section 2.5: Refining How You Respond

- *Make Your Stories Personal*: Including thought process and reflection gives stories depth beyond a list of events. They show how choices were evaluated, why actions were taken, and how those decisions influence the way responsibilities are approached today.

- *Highlight Emotional Intelligence*: Emphasize the emotions you experienced during key moments. Whether it's pride, excitement, or even the challenges you faced, these feelings connect you with the interviewer and show your ability to grow through experiences.

- *Show Growth and Adaptability*: Growth becomes most persuasive when it moves beyond "what happened" and into "how it changed your approach." Describe how setbacks pushed you to reconsider assumptions, refine your process, or question blind spots. By stating how those lessons influence your choices today, you position adaptability as a discipline that influences the reasoning behind the choices you make.

2.6: The Power of Practice

- *Refine Through Repetition*: Rehearsing your stories out loud helps you find the right words, pacing, and tone. This technique also allows you to eliminate filler words and unnecessary details, keeping your story engaging and focused on the aspects that best reflect your growth.

- *Strengthen Your Story*: Seeking feedback from friends, mentors, or online tools provides perspectives you may not see on your own. Their input helps you identify opportunities to refine your approach, turning your story into a stronger reflection of your experience.

2.7: From Insight to Action

- ***Adapting to Various Interview Formats***: Different interview settings highlight different aspects of communication. When you adjust
  how you present your experiences: condensing for time, expanding
  for depth, or clarifying for a panel, you show that adaptability allows
  you to adjust the scope of your response while still emphasizing the
  results you delivered.

Remember, your story is your strength. Each experience: every challenge,
every success, provides insight into how reasoning shaped responses and
how outcomes shaped perspective. Over time, these stories illustrate the progression from immediate choices toward broader perspective that influences
future decisions. Stories prove their strength when they show how lessons
from the past have become tools for the future.

> *The most powerful person in the world is the storyteller.* –
> Steve Jobs

Chapter Three

The Interview Playbook

"Every accomplishment starts with the decision to try." - John F. Kennedy

3.1 What to Expect in a Technical Interview

Technical interviews are a key part of the hiring process in fields such as software engineering, data science, and other engineering disciplines. Unlike general interviews, they are designed to measure the knowledge and skills you'll actually use on the job. These assessments emphasize your approach to technical challenges, apply technical concepts to practical scenarios, and communicate your reasoning in a clear, logical way. Success isn't based solely on arriving at the right answer; it also depends on how you frame the problem, the steps you take to work toward a solution, and your ability to and your ability to walk someone through the concept in terms others can understand.

Technical Interviews: What Matters Most

- *Coding*: Show how your code reflects the way you solve problems: structuring logic so it's easy to follow, simplifying where possible, and making your reasoning visible through the flow of decisions.

- *Problem-Solving*: Show how you turn challenges into workable solutions by showing the logic behind your decisions: how you analyzed the situation, what informed your choices, and how you adjusted along the way.

- *Algorithms*: Explain how you selected and applied algorithms to address specific challenges, showing why the method fit and how it improved the outcome.

- *System Design*: Show how you approach system design by making your decisions easy to understand: how scalability, reliability, and trade-offs influenced the architecture you created.

Preparation Strategies: Success in technical interviews depends on preparation as much as knowledge. These strategies will help you refine your problem-solving, coding, and analytical abilities in ways that reflect the expectations of real interviews.

- *Sharpen Your Technical Edge*: Use platforms like LeetCode to work through coding challenges that mirror common interview questions. Regular practice helps refine your coding skills while reinforcing systematic problem-solving.

- *Algorithm Foundations*: Build a strong understanding of algorithms and data structures through platforms like Udemy, or similar course providers. Once comfortable with practical applications, expand your depth by studying Introduction to Algorithms by Cormen et al. (commonly referred to as CLRS), a widely used reference in the field.

- *System Design Insights*: Senior-level interviews evaluate how well you design systems that can handle growth, maintain availability during outages, and balance trade-offs in performance and cost. *Designing Data-Intensive Applications* by Martin Kleppmann is a leading reference for topics like data modeling, scalability patterns, and consistency models. To practice applying these concepts, platforms such as Interview Kickstart offer mock interviews focused on system architecture, giving you the chance to explain and defend your design decisions under realistic conditions.

- **Soft Skills Matter**: Technical interviews also assess how you communicate ideas, collaborate with others, and adapt when faced with new challenges. Reflect on examples from your past experiences that show these strengths, and consider resources like John Sonmez's *Soft Skills: The Software Developer's Life Manual* for structured ways to build them further.

- **Diversify Your Study Techniques**: Use multiple formats to strengthen your preparation. The CodeNewbie podcast exposes you to real developer experiences, while freeCodeCamp webinars provide guided coding practice. Combining these perspectives builds both technical skill and professional awareness that interviewers value.

3.2 What to Expect in a Case Interview

Introduction to Case Interviews

In case interviews, you're asked to think like a consultant. Given a business scenario, you're expected to break it into manageable parts, apply quantitative reasoning, and weigh trade-offs before recommending a course of action. This format shows interviewers whether you can take a messy, real-world problem and translate it into a solution they can use.

Case Interview Format and Expectations

A case interview mirrors the work consultants and strategists do daily. You'll need to confirm the client's objective, break down the problem into its key areas, and test your assumptions with both qualitative reasoning and quantitative analysis. What interviewers value is the ability to move from incomplete information to a logical recommendation while communicating your process in a way others could act on.

Approaching the Case: Approaching a case scenario with a methodical process helps you turn ambiguity into a structured analysis that interviewers can follow.

- *Get on the Same Page*: Begin by confirming the case details with the interviewer. Asking targeted questions not only ensures you understand the client's goals but also shows that you don't rush into assumptions, a trait interviewers pay close attention to.

- *Break It Down*: Break the issue into specific areas you can examine individually. For instance, in a customer satisfaction case, you might analyze feedback processes, service speed, and product quality. A clear structure shows that you can take an ambiguous problem and organize it in a way that others can follow.

- *Gather Critical Information*: Identify the information that will actually influence your analysis, and work with the interviewer to obtain data such as revenue trends, market share, or customer behavior. Targeted requests indicate that you can separate critical drivers from background noise.

- *Evaluate and Consolidate*: Apply appropriate methods to the data you've collected. For example, when reviewing a project, examine the relevant metrics and milestones to create a comprehensive overview, allowing you to identify trends and areas where improvements can be made.

- *Recommend Next Steps*: Propose actionable solutions supported by evidence from your analysis. Strong recommendations highlight that you can narrow a complex problem to its core issues, commit to a direction that others can rely on, and support it with reasoning that would stand up in a client setting.

Practice Resources: Preparing for case interviews requires consistent practice to strengthen both your problem-solving process and your comfort with the interview format. Working through cases repeatedly helps you develop habits that interviewers measure: framing the problem clearly, prioritizing the areas with the greatest impact, testing assumptions with data, and explaining your reasoning step by step. Explore these resources to access case materials and practice opportunities:

- *Essential Reading for Case Interview Prep*: If you're preparing for case interviews, two of the most widely used resources are *Case in Point* by Marc P. Cosentino and *Case Interview Secrets* by Victor Cheng. Both provide structured methods and sample cases that reflect real interview expectations.

- *Peer-Powered Growth*: Practicing with peers exposes you to alternative frameworks and reasoning styles that you might not develop on your own. In group practice, one person might break down a profitability case by focusing on revenue streams, while another highlights cost drivers, giving everyone a broader toolkit for structuring future problems. This exchange also trains you to work with feedback, which reflects the collaborative mindset and flexibility expected in consulting and strategy roles.

- *Free Case Interview Resources*: Beyond books, there are platforms offering high-quality, no-cost preparation. Rocketblocks provides practice prompts and drills designed to sharpen core skills like mental math and hypothesis-driven analysis. Firm Learning breaks down real case scenarios step by step, helping you see how top candidates frame problems, focus on what influences the outcome, and communicate recommendations under interview conditions.

3.3 Industry-Specific Interview Prep

Understanding Your Industry's Expectations

Each industry has its own expectations, and it's normal to feel uncertain as you prepare for interviews. Whether you're looking at healthcare, education, the creative arts, or another field, focus on learning the basics that will help you speak the industry's language. Start by reading about current trends, common challenges, and the skills that employers emphasize in entry-level roles. Reach out to alumni, professors, or professionals for short conversations about their experiences, and use industry websites or beginner-friendly resources to deepen your understanding. This preparation equips you to ask relevant questions, translate your experiences into what employers in this area focus on, and present yourself as someone who can grow into the role while already thinking like a professional. As you prepare for conversations in your field, see Toolkit 5: Digital Footprint Workshop to ensure your online presence reflects your professional standards.

Strategic Skill Alignment: Interviewers value candidates who connect their background to the role. Here are ways to highlight your industry experience:

- *Align Your Experience to the Role*: Show how your past work connects directly to the role's requirements and the and the priorities of the teams doing this work. Interviewers are looking for evidence that you understand what the organization values and can contribute to it from day one.

- *Use Industry Language:* Incorporate terms and examples that professionals in the field expect. Using the right language shows fluency in the industry's culture and reassures interviewers that you'll adapt smoothly to their environment.

- *Show Ongoing Learning*: Highlight recent courses, certifications, or projects that prove you're keeping pace with changes in the work you want to do. This shows initiative and reassures employers you'll continue to grow with the field.

- *Ground Responses in Context*: When asked scenario-based questions, frame your solutions around the conditions teams are working with today. For example, in education you might suggest ways to strengthen student engagement in remote settings, showing that your recommendations are relevant, useful, and based on the challenges employers are actively managing.

3.4 Tech Talk, Simplified

In the tech world, clear communication makes your skills more visible. Here, you'll learn how to present technical ideas so they are understandable, persuasive, and valuable to interviewers regardless of their background.

Turning Tech into Talk: Explaining concepts from your field in a way that non-technical interviewers can follow is a skill that sets candidates apart. Analogies are especially effective because they translate abstract ideas into familiar experiences. Here's how to use them effectively:

Use Relatable Comparisons: Choose comparisons that simplify the idea without losing accuracy. A strong analogy shows that you can adapt your explanation to your audience, a quality interviewers actively look for.

- *Example*: Debugging software is like tracing a leak in a complex plumbing system. You methodically isolate sections until you find the source of the issue, the same way you test code blocks to locate the cause of the problem.

Focus on the 'Why': Start by explaining the value of the concept before diving into the technical details. Doing so gives your audience context and shows interviewers that you can connect technical work to its business impact.

- *Example*: Introducing cloud computing might begin with its benefits: scalability, reduced IT overhead, and improved collaboration. Once the value is clear, you can explain how services are deployed and managed.

Avoid Jargon: Use straightforward language instead of relying on technical shorthand. If specialized terms are necessary, explain them in plain words so interviewers of any background can follow your reasoning.

- *Example*: Instead of saying, "The software architecture was designed for high scalability," you could say, "We built the system so it can handle more users and data by adding resources as needed, without affecting performance.

Chunk Information: Break explanations into clear steps rather than presenting everything at once. In interviews, this shows that you can organize complex ideas logically and guide the listener through your reasoning.

- *Example*: Instead of saying, "An API facilitates communication between systems," you could explain it step by step: "First, think of an API as a menu in a restaurant. The menu lists options. Next, the kitchen prepares what you select. Finally, the waiter delivers it. Similarly, an API lists available operations, processes the request, and returns the result."

Connecting Through Conversation

Strong interviewers don't just listen to what you know, they pay attention to how you involve them in the discussion. Treating your explanation as a dialogue reflects collaboration, adaptability, and confidence in your expertise.

Make Explanations Interactive: Treat technical explanations as conversations, not monologues. Intentionally pause at key points to invite input: asking if the level of detail matches what the interviewer wants, or if they'd like you to expand on a step. This doesn't just give them space to respond; it shows you can read the room, adapt in real time, and respect their perspective. Interviewers notice when candidates create this two-way flow because it mirrors how effective communication works on teams: responsive, adaptive, and collaborative.

- *Example*: After walking through a performance optimization, you might say: "We identified that server latency was spiking during peak traffic. Before I move into how we solved it with caching, would it help if I explain the metrics we tracked to confirm it was a bottleneck?" This creates a checkpoint that keeps the discussion collaborative.

Present the Logic Behind the Work: When walking through technical projects, don't just state what you did, make the thinking behind your choices visible. Show how you assessed the problem, the alternatives you considered, and why you chose a particular path. Breaking your explanation into stages shows the structure of your thinking and demonstrates that your choices were deliberate rather than reactive. This approach reassures interviewers that your process is systematic and transferable to future challenges.

- *Example*: When describing a data pipeline fix, you could explain: "I mapped failure points across the system logs, ran controlled tests to isolate the bottleneck, and then reconfigured the load balancer." Explaining the sequence shows the method behind the solution.

Share What Drives Your Interest: Enthusiasm has the greatest impact when tied to concrete achievements. Rather than stating that you enjoy your work, show where your excitement came alive in a technical challenge you overcame, an innovative approach you introduced, or a measurable result you helped deliver. When you connect your energy to something tangible, interviewers see both your passion and your ability to produce results, making the impression more credible and lasting.

- *Example*: Instead of just mentioning your interest, say, "When I explain how we designed our cloud infrastructure, I do it with real enthusiasm. Creating a system that scales effortlessly and knowing it can handle anything we throw at it, it's what I love about cloud engineering."

Connect Solutions to Impact: Tie your technical work to the benefits it created for the team, the project, or the organization. Show how your technical contributions produced outcomes that others valued: whether by improving efficiency, reducing risks, saving costs, or enabling growth. This shows your ability to frame technical outcomes in terms of risk reduction, financial return, or strategic advantage.

- *Example*: Instead of saying, "I wrote a script for data entry," you could say, "I created an automated data entry script that reduced errors and saved the team hours each week, allowing them to focus more on reviewing client information and helping customers."

3.5 Turning Feedback into Growth

Each interview gives you something to build on, and those lessons drive your growth. When you reflect on what worked and what didn't, you strengthen how well you tie your experiences to the role and how effectively you adjust when the conversation moves in new directions. With each reflection, you refine your judgment, recognizing which details support your message and which distract, a skill that can change the impact of every answer.

Structured Practice: You don't discover your blind spots by reviewing in isolation, you find them when practice mirrors the pressure of the real thing.

- *What to Do*: Block practice sessions on your calendar and protect that time as you would a professional obligation. Use mock interviews, timed case questions, or role-play exercises with a peer to rehearse in a format that reflects the interview environment. Run the session start to finish without pausing or restarting: this exposes gaps in preparation, strengthens your timing, and builds the ability to recover when pressure disrupts your delivery.

- *Why It Matters*: Pressure changes how you think and speak. It strips away the comfort of preparation and shows how you perform when decisions must be made on the spot. Practicing in that environment strengthens skills that interviews measure directly: organizing your thoughts quickly, explaining your reasoning in clear steps, and building the discipline to keep discussions productive and outcome-driven. Those same skills become strengths you'll rely on in your career: they shape the way you contribute in meetings, present ideas, and earn credibility when others look to you for direction.

Progress Through Feedback: Feedback isn't just advice, it's what turns practice into real progress. It's the difference between practicing and actually improving.

- *What to Do*: After each practice session, set aside a few minutes to review it with someone you trust. Ask them to comment on three areas: how easy your points were to follow, whether your reasoning was easy to follow, and how confident your delivery sounded. Write their feedback down, pay attention to any recurring themes, and decide one adjustment you'll test in your next session. For guidance on requesting feedback that helps you understand how your responses came across, see Toolkit 3: Feedback Request Template.

- *Why It Matters*: Feedback shows the difference between your intended message and the impression it created. It shows if your pacing left the impression of being rushed, if your reasoning was too compressed to follow, or if your examples failed to highlight the skills the role requires. Acting on that feedback ensures the skills you want noticed (whether technical expertise, problem-solving, or teamwork) are the same ones the interviewer actually takes away.

Improving with Every Interview: Each interview provides a unique learning opportunity. Reflecting on what you've experienced helps you refine how you prepare for the next conversation.

- *What to Do*: After the interview, review what actually happened, not what you hoped would happen. Did your introduction set the interviewer up to see the relevance of your background? Were your examples detailed enough to show decision-making and results, or did they describe the situation but fail to connect it to the skills the interviewer is evaluating? Did you confirm what the interviewer was really asking, or did you respond with information that left the original concern unresolved? If you want guidance as you review how your interviews progressed and what they suggest for future practice, see Toolkit 4: Post-Interview Analysis Template.

- *Why It Matters*: Without this kind of reflection, you risk repeating the same weaknesses in every interview. By analyzing where your explanation left gaps, such as overlooking the result of the situation or not bringing your answer back to the role, you build a record of what limits your performance; this gives you direction for your next round of preparation. Addressing those issues interview by interview means your answers show the interviewer how you approach problems, what actions you take, and what results you deliver.

3.6 Staying Calm Under Pressure

Stress in an interview doesn't just affect how you feel, it changes what the interviewer takes away. Speaking too quickly can make valuable experience sound unfocused. Skipping steps in your reasoning can make decisions seem incomplete. Closing without linking back to the role can make your skills difficult to recognize. Managing those situations ensures the interviewer sees the full picture of your abilities, not a reduced version constrained by pressure.

Stress Management Techniques: Stress often shows up in interviews as racing thoughts, shallow breathing, or nervous habits. With the right tools, you can reduce those distractions and bring your full attention to the discussion.

- *What to Do*: Before the interview, try a simple breathing exercise: inhale through your nose for four counts, hold briefly, then exhale through your mouth for six counts, repeating for a few minutes to calm your body. You can also practice mindfulness by focusing on your breath and gently returning your attention whenever your mind drifts, even for just five minutes. Progressive muscle relaxation is another option: tense each muscle group for five seconds, then release for ten, starting at your toes and working upward. After the interview, using these same techniques can steady your focus, making it easier to replay key moments and capture insights while they're still fresh.

- *Why It Matters*: Using techniques like deep breathing, mindfulness, and muscle relaxation reduces physical tension and mental distraction, giving you more control over your pace, tone, and delivery during the interview.

Responding to Unexpected Questions: One of the hardest moments in an interview arrives when you're asked something you didn't anticipate. In that moment, your ability to pause, frame your answer, and explain your reasoning shows more about your potential than rehearsed responses ever could.

- *What to Do*: If a question catches you off guard, give yourself a moment before speaking instead of rushing into an answer. Begin with your main point in one or two sentences, then explain the reasoning behind it or add a short example to illustrate your thinking. For instance, if asked about handling conflict, you might say, "I approach conflict by identifying common goals early, so both sides see we're working toward the same outcome." The structure helps the interviewer see both your conclusion and the logic behind it, giving them confidence in how you approach real challenges.

- *Why It Matters*: When you lead with your main idea, the interviewer doesn't have to wait through background details to understand your point. Following up with reasoning or an example then shows how you reached that conclusion, which makes your answer both clear and credible.

3.7 Wrap-Up: The Interview Playbook

As you close this chapter, take a moment to recognize how much you've added to your toolkit. You've explored techniques that prepare you to handle both the expected and the unexpected with greater confidence in your approach. These skills will serve you well by helping you provide answers that are direct, well-structured, and easier for the interviewer to act on.

Key Takeaways

Section 3.1: What to Expect in a Technical Interview

- *Code with Confidence*: Your code should make your logic easy to follow and your solutions easy to verify. Practicing regularly builds that consistency, so when you present your work, it reflects both your ability and your preparation.

- *Explaining Your Approach Matters*: In many interviews, the process matters more than the solution itself. Explaining your reasoning shows the interviewer that you can analyze a problem, weigh alternatives, and make decisions based on sound judgment.

- *Team Player Qualities*: Interviews often reveal whether you can collaborate, not just whether you can solve problems alone. Demonstrating respect for others' input and building on their ideas shows you can work within a team to reach stronger solutions.

Section 3.2: What to Expect in a Case Interview

- *Structure Over Speed*: When faced with a case interview, don't rush straight into calculations or guesses. Start by clarifying the details, then outline the areas you'll examine; like costs, customer behavior, or process steps. Working through each area in order shows the interviewer you can structure your thinking and avoid overlooking key components.

- *Stay Curious*: In a case interview, ask questions that fill in missing details: who the customer is, what resources are available, or what constraints will have the biggest impact. Exploring these specifics shows the interviewer that you examine assumptions instead of working with incomplete information.

Section 3.3: Industry-Specific Interview Prep

- *Aligning Strengths with Opportunity*: In an interview, connect your past experience directly to what the role requires. Pointing out how your skills address the job's key responsibilities shows the interviewer you understand their needs and are able to contribute to the team right away.

Section 3.4: Tech Talk, Simplified

- *Speak Their Language*: In technical interviews, simplify complex ideas by using plain language and straightforward examples. Comparing a system or process to something familiar, like traffic flow or assembling a puzzle, helps the interviewer follow your reasoning even if they don't share your technical background.

Section 3.5: Turning Feedback into Growth

- *Prepare with Purpose*: Practice interview questions the same way you'll face them: out loud, under time limits, and without notes. Rehearsing in this format helps you practice communicating in a way that is easy for the interviewer to follow, even when the question is challenging.

- *Feedback Fuels Progress*: Don't stop at listening to feedback, act on it. If you're told an answer was too long, practice trimming it to 90 seconds. If you seemed uncertain, rehearse saying your main point first. Targeting feedback in this way builds noticeable improvement.

Section 3.6: Staying Calm Under Pressure

- *Stress Management Techniques*: Right before the interview starts, inhale through your nose for four counts, hold for two, and exhale through your mouth for six. This lowers tension and helps you start your answers with a calmer, more controlled tone.

- *Responding to Unexpected Questions*: Don't rush into answering a tough question. Take a moment to collect your thoughts, state your conclusion first, and then share the reasoning behind it. Interviewers notice this structure, it shows you can stay composed and give an answer that reflects both judgment and reasoning.

When an interview begins, preparation becomes visible in subtle ways: a pause before answering, attention held through eye contact, and framing responses around the central idea. These behaviors reflect structured preparation and allow interviewers to evaluate both the content of the response and the discipline behind it. Remember, the awareness gained in this chapter is transferable: each habit becomes part of a broader pattern of growth that strengthens communication, sharpens reasoning, and reinforces professional presence.

"Success is the result of preparation, hard work, and learning from failure." – Colin Powell

Chapter Four

Interview Chemistry 101

> *"The most important thing in communication is hearing what isn't said."* – Peter Drucker

4.1 The Art of Engagement

The impression you create in an interview comes from both your words and your presence. How you express enthusiasm for the role and the company can be seen in your communication and in the subtleties of body language. What you may not realize is how small adjustments in posture, tone, or phrasing can change the entire direction of a conversation.

Fully Present, Fully Engaged: Active engagement during an interview begins with being fully present. Eye contact, open body language, paying close attention to the interviewer's perspective, and showing authentic interest through your responses all contribute to the impression you make. Together, these actions create a sense of connection that shows you're invested in the conversation.

- *What to Do*: Sit upright with your shoulders in a natural position to avoid appearing tense. Keep eye contact natural, shifting briefly when needed so it doesn't feel forced. Use small gestures, such as nodding or leaning in slightly, to show you are following the conversation. Silence your phone and avoid fidgeting. When the interviewer mentions something relevant, connect it to a skill, project, or situation from your experience to show the conversation has your full attention.

- *Why It Matters*: Interviews are shaped as much by connection as by information. When your stories, tone, and body language work together, they create a more complete picture of who you are. Your presence and interest can outweigh brief uncertainty, reinforcing the impact you make. Engagement conveys attentiveness to both the conversation and the relationship, leaving the interviewer with a clearer sense of who you are.

Making Your Case: Strong answers in an interview show that you under-stand the role and can connect it to what you bring to the table. The goal is to make it easy for the interviewer to see how your skills and experiences fit their needs.

- *What to Do*: As you hear each question, think about what the inter-viewer is really trying to understand. Pause briefly before respond-ing, then select a specific example that illustrates the skill or quality behind the question. Use a simple structure: describe the situation, outline your role, and explain the outcome. Keep the focus on what you contributed and what you learned, this shows both competence and growth.

- *Why It Matters*: Well-structured answers reduce the interviewer's guesswork. They make it easier for them to connect your background to the role and to justify why you should advance in the process. Strong answers also give the interviewer material they can use to advocate for you when discussing candidates with their team. Re-member, the more directly you show how your experiences fit their needs, the less room there is for doubt.

4.2 Smart Questions, Strong Impression

The questions you ask at the end of an interview influence how the conversation closes and how you are remembered. Strong questions show that you've researched the role, thought about the company's direction, and can connect your interests to their needs. They also give the interviewer material that reinforces you as someone who prepares, listens, and engages strategically. This section will show you how to build questions that leave a lasting impression while giving you useful insight into the role.

Asking Questions with Purpose: In an interview, the questions you ask shape how interviewers interpret your readiness for the role. They pay attention to whether your questions reflect an understanding of what it takes to meet expectations once the work begins, not just what it takes to secure an offer.

- *What to Do*: As you prepare, think about where expectations are likely to be unclear at the start of the role. Direct your questions toward how performance is evaluated early on, how work is prioritized when multiple requests compete for attention, and how feedback is typically handled when adjustments are needed. Avoid questions that simply confirm public information. Focus on questions that would change how you prepare for the role if the answer were different.

- *Why It Matters*: The questions you ask give interviewers information they can't get from your résumé or prepared responses. They show how you interpret expectations, how you think about early responsibility, and what you pay attention to when information is incomplete. In hiring discussions, this often becomes a reference point. Interviewers use your questions to reason about how you would approach the role once expectations are no longer being explicitly stated.

Asking the Right Questions: Developing strong questions comes down to two things: preparing through research and focusing on what you need to know to evaluate the role. The more specific your questions, the more they highlight your preparation and seriousness about the opportunity.

- *What to Do*: Build a short list of questions that connect directly to what you've learned about the company. Instead of defaulting to generic questions, center them on areas that matter most to you: how the team works, how progress is evaluated, and what the company prioritizes for the future. For instance, you might ask how your manager supports training for new hires, how early expectations are communicated, or how different departments share updates when working on the same project. Keep your questions open-ended to encourage detail, but targeted enough to show you've taken the time to understand the organization.

- *Why It Matters*: The questions you ask give the interviewer a window into how you think. By preparing focused questions, you show that you're evaluating the role with the same thoroughness the company is evaluating you. This shifts the interview from one-sided evaluation to a two-way conversation. The answers help you decide whether the culture and expectations align with what you want, a critical part of making a sound career decision.

4.3 Questions by Focus Area

The questions you ask in an interview should help you gather specifics you can't find on a website or job description. Ask in ways that show you want to understand how success in the role is measured, what the team's day-to-day work looks like, and how managers support their staff. These kinds of questions give you real information about how the company operates and whether it matches what you need to do your best work. In this section, you'll find examples, organized by focus areas, that you can adapt to leave the interview with concrete details about performance expectations, management style, and workplace culture.

Company Culture and Values: Culture isn't about what's written on a website; it's about how people treat each other and how leaders act during high-pressure deadlines, unexpected setbacks, or team conflicts. Asking about these areas helps you see whether the company operates in a way that matches how you want to work.

- **What to Ask**: "How do team members typically support each other during busy or high-pressure periods?" or "Can you describe a time when the team faced a tough situation and how they handled it together?"

- **Why It Matters**: These questions give you a look at the behavior behind the company's values. They show whether teamwork is real, how challenges are handled, and whether leaders and employees act in ways that line up with what the company says it believes. The answers give you evidence you can use to decide whether this is an environment where you'll be supported and able to succeed.

Role-Specific Questions: Job descriptions often give only a high-level overview. To know whether a position is truly the right fit, you need to understand what the day-to-day work looks like, what projects take priority, and how challenges are handled. Asking role-specific questions gives you a realistic picture of the responsibilities you'd take on and the expectations you'd be measured against.

- *What to Ask*: "Can you describe a typical project I might work on?" or "What are the most significant challenges this position currently faces?"

- *Why It Matters*: These questions clarify how your time would actually be spent, the challenges you'd face, and the standards you'd be held to. The answers give you a realistic basis to decide whether the role plays to your strengths and matches the type of work you want.

Team and Collaboration: The people you work with influence your success as much as the responsibilities of the role itself. Team dynamics affect whether workloads are shared fairly, whether conflicts are addressed constructively, and whether collaboration helps you achieve more or slows you down. Asking about these areas gives you a realistic view of what it's like to work on this team.

- *What to Ask*: "Can you share an example of how the team navigated a recent challenge or conflict?" or "How does management encourage collaboration and support both individual and team development?"

- *Why It Matters*: These questions give you specifics you can't get from a job description. The answers highlight whether teamwork is dependable during busy periods, whether conflict resolution builds trust or creates tension, and whether managers invest time in developing their teams. This helps you judge whether the team would give you the support and environment you need to succeed.

Motivation and Performance: How a company motivates its people and recognizes their work shows a lot about the culture. It shows whether effort is valued, how success is celebrated, and how the organization keeps employees engaged. Asking about these areas helps you see if recognition is a regular part of the workplace or an afterthought.

- *What to Ask*: "Can you share an example of how the team's hard work was recognized recently?" or "How does the company usually show appreciation for team successes?"

- *Why It Matters*: These questions give you evidence of whether recognition is consistent, whether appreciation comes from leadership or peers, and how much value is placed on employee effort. The answers help you judge if this is an environment where good work is noticed, contributions are rewarded, and motivation is supported, conditions that directly affect your engagement and long-term satisfaction.

Company Pride and Satisfaction: When employees talk about what makes them proud to work at a company, they often point to the factors that carry the most weight: how the organization treats its people, the impact of its work, and the moments that make employees want to stay. Asking about pride helps you see which aspects of the culture employees value most and whether those same factors would be important to you.

- *What to Ask*: "What do you love most about working here?" or "Can you share a moment that truly made you feel like this is the right place for you?"

- *Why It Matters*: These questions provide insight into what employees truly appreciate about the company, from growth opportunities to how success is shared. Their answers help you judge whether the environment encourages the kind of pride and satisfaction you want in your career.

Work Environment Dynamics: The work environment affects how tasks are divided, how progress is tracked, and how people interact throughout the day. Knowing whether the company relies more on collaboration or independent work gives you a realistic picture of what your daily routine would look like and how you'd fit into the team.

- *What to Ask*: "Can you tell me more about the work environment? Does it lean more towards collaboration or working independently?"

- *Why It Matters*: These questions give you a clear view of how work is organized: whether projects are handled through group problem-solving or individual ownership, how communication flows, and what level of accountability is expected. The answers help you see if the company's approach matches the way you work best.

Tools and Technology Utilization: The tools you'll be expected to use say a lot about the company's approach to innovation. Up-to-date systems can make it easier to learn, adapt, and grow in your career, while outdated tools can hold you back. By asking about technology, you gain a clear view of whether the company invests in systems that support both your work today and your development over time.

- *What to Ask*: "Can you tell me about the tools and technologies the team uses?" or "Are there any new systems or platforms the company is planning to adopt soon?"

- *Why It Matters*: Asking about tools helps you see how the company equips people to do their jobs. You'll learn if processes run smoothly, if collaboration is supported, and if there are opportunities to strengthen your skills through technology. This information helps you judge whether the role sets you up for success or for frustration.

Interdepartmental Collaboration: How a team works with other departments tells you a lot about the company's communication style and overall approach to teamwork. Understanding these interactions helps you see whether the organization encourages knowledge sharing or operates in silos.

- *What to Ask*: "How often does your team collaborate with other departments, and what does that collaboration typically involve for someone in this role?" or "Can you share an example of a recent cross-departmental project and how the teams worked together?"

- *Why It Matters*: The answers show whether the company shares knowledge openly, resolves conflicts constructively, and uses collaboration to create learning opportunities. This gives you a clear sense of whether you'd be joining a culture that builds momentum or one slowed down by barriers between teams.

Early Performance Expectations: Knowing what the company expects in your first few months helps you focus on the right priorities from day one. Clear expectations show you how your work will be evaluated, what support you'll receive, and how quickly the organization expects you to contribute.

- *What to Ask*: "What are the key performance expectations for this role in the first 6 to 12 months?" or "How will my success be evaluated during the onboarding period?"

- *Why It Matters*: These questions show you what the company prioritizes in the first months: deadlines, skills, or results, and how your performance will be measured. The answers give you specific evidence of whether the role aligns with your strengths and how much support you can expect.

Identifying Role Challenges: Challenges are often what make or break someone's experience in a role. Understanding them upfront helps you avoid surprises, prepare for the demands, and decide whether the position fits your strengths. Asking about challenges can show whether the job requires balancing competing priorities, managing a heavy workload, or building skills in areas that need extra focus.

- *What to Ask*: "In your experience, what are the most demanding aspects of this role?" or "What challenges have past team members faced in this position?"

- *Why It Matters*: These questions highlight the parts of the job that are most likely to challenge you day to day. The answers show you whether those challenges align with your strengths or fall in areas you'll need to develop. They also give you a clear picture of the role's toughest aspects so you can walk in knowing what to expect, rather than being surprised after you start.

Growth and Development: How a company develops its people shows you whether they invest in long-term success or simply focus on immediate results. Asking about training, feedback, and advancement opportunities helps you see how talent is supported and whether you'll have room to grow in the role.

- **What to Ask**: "What kind of growth and learning opportunities can I expect in this role?" or "How often does the team receive feedback on their performance, and what does that process look like?"

- **Why It Matters**: These questions point to how development actually happens: whether through structured training, regular feedback, or clear advancement paths. The answers give you evidence of how the company supports learning, how performance is evaluated, and whether you'll have the resources and guidance to keep progressing in your career.

4.4 Questions That Work for You

The way you ask questions can change the tone of an interview. Well-timed and well-phrased questions show that you're listening attentively, give the interviewer a chance to share useful insights, and turn the exchange into a conversation that works both ways. In this section, you'll learn how to recognize the best moments to ask, and how to frame your questions so they draw out detailed answers that help you evaluate both the role and the organization.

Start Broad, Get Specific: Strong questions move from general to focused. Begin by understanding the company's mission, culture, and priorities, then narrow in on how those connect to the role you're pursuing. This approach gives you both the big picture and a clear sense of how your work would fit into it.

- *What to Do*: Open with broad questions about the company's overall goals or challenges, then move to specifics by asking how the role fits into that context. For instance, you might ask, "What priorities is the company focusing on this quarter?" followed by, "How would my role directly support those priorities?"

- *Why It Matters*: This approach helps you connect the company's big-picture priorities to what your daily work would actually look like. It also shows you what the company will expect from you in the role and whether those expectations align with the way you work best.

Questions that Encourage Openness: The way you phrase your questions often determines the kind of answers you'll receive. Open, respectful wording invites interviewers to share more detail and creates a conversation that feels less scripted. This helps you gain insight to information you wouldn't get from yes-or-no questions.

- *What to Do*: Phrase your questions so they encourage explanation rather than defensiveness. Keep your tone respectful and focus on learning, not judging. For example, instead of asking about a problem directly, you could ask, "What's something the team is currently working to improve, and how are they approaching it?" Or, "What recent change has been the most positive for the team?"

- *Why It Matters*: These questions bring out details you won't find in a job description, such as how leaders handle challenges and how priorities are set. The answers give you evidence to decide whether the company communicates openly, explains decisions clearly, and operates with transparency employees can trust.

4.5 Reading the Room

The way an interviewer answers your questions tells you as much about the role as your resume tells them about you. Listen for how managers describe supporting their teams, how challenges are explained, and how priorities are set. These responses can show you if deadlines are achievable, if managers explain priorities in a way people can act on, and if the role is designed to set employees up for success. This section will help you identify those indicators and decide whether the role provides the conditions you need to succeed.

Stay Present, Stay Connected: How you listen in an interview affects what you learn. By staying fully present, you can pick up details about how the role is viewed, what the company prioritizes, and how the interviewer communicates about both. These cues show how work actually gets done, from communication style to priorities, helping determine whether the environment provides the conditions needed for success.

- *What to Do*: Listen not only to the interviewer's words but also to the tone, emphasis, and pace they use. Notice if they speak with enthusiasm about certain aspects of the role, hesitate when discussing challenges, or provide detail in some areas while downplaying others. Employers often minimize topics that may be sensitive: high turnover, unclear expectations, or resource constraints. It's worth asking clarifying questions. Use these observations to ask follow-up questions that show you're engaged and give you a clearer view of the role's responsibilities and challenges.

- *Why It Matters*: This approach shows you how leaders communicate, whether they value transparency, and what they emphasize as most important. The specifics they mention: budgets, staffing levels, training, or support structures, give you a realistic sense of whether the role is set up for success or if resources will be a struggle.

Reading Between the Lines: What interviewers choose to highlight in their answers often tells you as much as the job description itself. Pay attention to the details they share about how decisions are made, how feedback is given, and how the team works together. These responses give you a clearer picture of what daily life in the role looks like and how the company functions beyond its polished description.

- *What to Do*: Listen closely when interviewers describe how the team works. If they mention collaboration, ask follow-up questions to understand whether teamwork happens through open discussion, scheduled meetings, or individual accountability. Take note of specific tools or systems they reference, such as project management platforms or communication channels. Then, think about how these practices match your preferred way of working and the environments where you've been most effective.

- *Why It Matters*: The way a team communicates and makes decisions directly affects your daily experience. Direct answers show whether this is a structured environment with defined processes or one that relies on flexibility and individual initiative. They also give you a sense of how collaboration influences relationships within the team: supportive, independent, or somewhere in between.

4.6 Taking It to the Next Level

Asking follow-up questions during an interview demonstrates that you're listening closely and processing what's being said. It shows you can build on information in real time, turning the exchange into a two-way discussion rather than a list of prepared questions. This section will show you how to ask follow-up questions that build directly on the interviewer's responses, helping you learn more about expectations, priorities, and how the role contributes to the team.

Smart Follow-Up Moves: When you ask follow-up questions, you show the interviewer that you value their input and are actively engaging with what they've shared. It makes the discussion more collaborative and gives them a sense of how you would communicate as part of the team.

- *What to Do*: If the interviewer mentions a project, ask what challenges the team faced, how they addressed unexpected obstacles, and what they learned from the experience. These follow-ups show that you're interested in how the team works through problems, not just the end results.

- *Why It Matters*: Follow-up questions show that you're listening actively and capable of drawing insight from what's shared in real time. They often expose how priorities are set, how teams respond when plans shift, and how decisions are communicated. For you, this provides a clearer sense of what daily work would involve; for the interviewer, it highlights how you approach complex topics with curiosity, structure, and focus.

Think of the Interview as a Conversation: Viewing the interview as a conversation changes how you participate. Instead of giving one-sided answers, you ask follow-up questions, build on what the interviewer shares, and create a back-and-forth that feels natural. This approach highlights skills hiring managers rely on every day: the ability to listen carefully, respond with relevance, and move discussions toward outcomes.

- *What to Do*: Approach follow-up questions as part of the dialogue rather than a checklist. When the interviewer mentions a project or challenge, ask how it affects the role you're applying for, what the team learned from it, or how success is measured. Keep each question tied to the job and company so the discussion stays focused.

- *Why It Matters*: A conversational approach shows that you can pick up on cues, adjust your responses, and stay engaged without relying on a script. This adaptability is valuable in real work settings where discussions rarely follow a predictable outline.

4.7 Wrap-Up: Interview Chemistry 101

As we bring this chapter to a close, it's important to see interview success for what it really is: the ability to show how you think, how you solve problems, and how you interact in real time. Employers are evaluating whether you can explain your experience in a way that connects to their needs, whether you can adapt when a question takes an unexpected turn, and whether you create an exchange that feels productive rather than rehearsed. In the next section, we'll revisit the strategies you've worked through: from active listening to role-specific questioning, so you can apply them to connect your experience directly to the problems this role is designed to solve.

Key Takeaways:

Section 4.1: The Art of Engagement

- *Fully Present, Fully Engaged*: Engagement shows through details: consistent eye contact, an open posture, and small cues like nodding when you follow a point. These behaviors allow the interviewer to gauge how engaged you are with their questions and whether you're fully involved in the discussion.

- *Making Your Case:* Interviewers listen for how your background translates into what the role requires. Instead of speaking in general terms, point to specific moments: finishing a project under a tight deadline, coordinating with another department, or solving a recurring problem in your past role. These examples give the interviewer clear evidence of how your skills apply to the challenges of the position.

Section 4.2: Smart Questions, Strong Impression

- *Emphasize Your Value*: When you ask about how success is measured or what the team is working toward, you show that you're already thinking about how your skills can meet those expectations. This tells the interviewer you're evaluating where you can contribute to their priorities, not just where you might fit on the org chart.

- *Align with the Role*: Shape your responses around the skills and experiences the job description emphasizes: problem-solving, collaboration, or managing deadlines. Doing this shows the interviewer that you've studied the role, understand what it requires, and can point to evidence from your background that matches their needs. The more directly you connect your experiences to the position, the easier it is for the interviewer to understand the specific value you could bring to the team.

Section 4.3: Questions by Focus Area

- *Comprehensive Insight*: Asking questions about culture, daily responsibilities, team dynamics, performance expectations, and opportunities for development gives you a detailed picture of what working in the role would actually look like. This information helps you judge how the job matches the way you prefer to work, the skills you want to use, and the kind of environment where you can continue to grow.

Section 4.4: Questions That Work For You

- *Ask to Understand, Not Just to Ask*: When you ask questions that push past yes-or-no answers, such as how performance is measured in the first six months or how the team shares updates during a project, you show that you're interested in the realities of the role. This approach not only gives you useful details about expectations and workflows but also shows the interviewer that you're focused on how you would operate within their environment.

Section 4.5: Reading the Room

- *Listen Well, Learn More*: Pay attention to the specifics in an interviewer's words and tone: mentions of tight deadlines, team support, or leadership style often tell you more than the job posting. Picking up on these cues helps you judge the realities of the role and prepare better follow-up questions.

- *Consider the Culture*: Pay attention to what the interviewer's answers show about how people work together, how leaders make decisions, and how employees are supported. These details show you what daily life in the organization is really like. You'll walk away knowing how the company operates day to day: in the way people communicate, handle conflict, and recognize contributions.

Section 4.6: Taking It to the Next Level

- *Listen, Understand, Engage*: Active listening and follow-up questions show that you can pick up details, connect them to what you already know, and respond in ways that link the discussion back to the responsibilities of the position. This demonstrates skills the interviewer is looking for: the ability to process information, identify priorities, and add value in collaborative discussions.

- *Interview Flow*: Treating the interview as a dialogue allows the interviewer to observe how you think rather than just what you say. The way you ask clarifying questions, expand on a point, or link one idea to another demonstrates how you process information in real time. This matters because employers want insight into your reasoning process, not just your final answer.

As we close out this chapter, remember that every response and follow-up offers the interviewer evidence of how you'll perform in the role. When you explain how you resolved a conflict, clarify a detail they raise, or expand on a project you led, you're showing them your judgment, adaptability, and approach to teamwork. What they leave with isn't just your resume, it's a picture of the value you could add to their team.

"Listening is an art that requires attention over talent, spirit over ego, and others over self." – Dean Jackson

Chapter Five

Interactive Interviewing

"What you do today can improve all your tomorrows." – Ralph Marston

5.1 Boost Your Impact Post-Interview

An interview does not end when you leave the room. What follows is an opportunity to extend the impression you've made, reinforce your interest, and learn from the experience. Each interaction adds to your understanding of how you present yourself, how your responses are received, and what you might strengthen for the future. This section brings together the steps of professional follow-up and the lessons gained through reflection, helping you recognize patterns, strengthen your approach, and enter your next interview with greater perspective.

Gratitude and Growth: Sending a thank-you note shows that you value the opportunity as much as the conversation itself. It reinforces your interest, shows professionalism in how you respect both the people and the process, and acknowledges the time given to you. Reflection helps you see the strategies that served you well and the habits that need refinement.

- *What to Do*: Within 24 hours, send a thank-you email to your primary contact, often HR or the hiring manager. Reference specific points from the conversation to show how you understood what was discussed and to reinforce your interest in the role. If you'd like support writing your thank-you email, see Toolkit 2: Thank-You Email Template. Express appreciation for the opportunity and the insights offered. Afterward, take time to think about your experience. Which parts of the conversation played to your strengths? Which parts of the interview showed the benefit of your preparation?

- *Why It Matters*: A thank-you note reframes the interview as a professional exchange rather than a one-sided evaluation. It reinforces your interest while leaving interviewers with a clear impression of your professionalism. Reflection shifts the focus from a single outcome to the development of long-term habits, helping you recognize how you present yourself, handle challenges, and adjust your preparation for future conversations.

Review and Refine: Reflection is what turns an interview from a single event into a source of learning. It allows you to see which parts of your preparation directly influenced the outcome, while also recognizing areas that need change without becoming caught up in what didn't go as planned.

- *What to Do*: After the interview, take time to think through the choices you made in the conversation. Which examples did you share, and how well did they fit the questions asked? Where did you feel your answers showed the preparation you put in, and where did you rely on quick thinking? Write down parts of the interview you would approach differently next time, as well as points you may want to raise in future discussions. If you'd like a structured way to review how your choices influenced the conversation, see Toolkit 4: Post-Interview Analysis Template.

- *Why It Matters*: Reflection shifts the interview from being only about the outcome to being part of a broader process. It shows you how your preparation supported you, how your answers came across, how you managed challenging questions, and where targeted adjustments could make your overall approach feel more consistent.

5.2 Growth Through Feedback

Requesting Actionable Feedback: Not all feedback is useful. The value comes from deciding what to do with it once you have it. Some comments will confirm strengths you should keep building on, while others may point to parts of your delivery that could be improved. Progress comes from distinguishing between feedback that validates your current approach and feedback that exposes gaps you might otherwise miss.

- *What to Do*: When you receive feedback, start by looking for patterns rather than reacting to single observations. Pay attention to themes that repeat or that reinforce what you've heard before. Turn the feedback into a short list of priorities, separating what you can strengthen now from what will require more practice over time.

- *Why It Matters*: Engaging with feedback this way keeps you from treating every observation as equally important. It directs your attention to adjustments that add value to your development and ensures those changes stay connected to the roles you're pursuing. Remember, the value of feedback lies in how you apply it to future opportunities.

Implementing Feedback: Feedback shows you the difference between intention and perception. By applying feedback, you begin to replace habits that undermine the impression you want to leave with approaches that make your strengths more visible to others.

- *What to Do*: Start by linking each piece of feedback to a specific part of your interview. If feedback suggests your examples felt too general, refine them with details that show your role and impact more clearly. If it points to pacing, rehearse under time limits until your delivery feels both complete and focused. When feedback raises questions about how you came across, test different ways of framing your responses with a mentor or peer until the strengths you want to emphasize come through. Remember, the value of feedback comes from turning it into specific changes that respond directly to the observations shared with you.

- *Why It Matters*: Acting on feedback teaches you to separate general advice from observations that consistently affect outcomes. That distinction lets you recognize how adjustments influence results, turning feedback into proof rather than opinion.

5.3 The Follow-Up Formula

Your interview doesn't end when you leave the room. What you do afterward can reinforce, or weaken, the impression you've made. Following up is not about sending messages for the sake of visibility, it is about showing that you understand timing, context, and professionalism. In this section, we'll look at how to handle follow-up in a way that strengthens your candidacy, keeps you engaged in the process, and shows respect for the employer's time.

Smart Follow-Up Moves: Once the interview ends, uncertainty can set in. The way you handle this stage reflects your judgment, showing whether you stay engaged without losing perspective.

- *What to Do*: If the interviewer provided a timeline and it has passed without an update, send a concise message that thanks them for the conversation and reaffirms your interest in the role. Strengthen your note by tying one of your qualifications to a point raised in the interview, such as a project, challenge, or team priority. Keep the email focused on reinforcing fit rather than repeating your resume or introducing unrelated details. After that, follow up only at appropriate points in the process, when a stated deadline has passed or when you're asked to provide additional information so your communication remains deliberate rather than repetitive.

- *Why It Matters*: How you handle the silence after an interview reflects the discipline you bring to professional interactions. A timely follow-up shows that you can stay engaged while respecting the structure of the hiring process. Employers read this as evidence of how you would manage unfinished work, navigate waiting periods in projects, and maintain communication when outcomes are outside your direct control.

When Silence is Loud: Delays in hearing back are common, but they also test whether you can combine persistence with respect for process.

- *What to Do*: If you don't receive a response, wait another week or two before sending a final follow-up. Keep your message brief yet professional: reaffirm your interest in the role, thank them for the time already provided, then ask whether there are additional steps you can take. Use this note to briefly highlight one qualification or experience that reinforces your fit. Mention that you remain available for further discussion. After sending, avoid further outreach. Setting this boundary shows persistence while maintaining professionalism, giving the employer the opportunity to complete their process.

- *Why It Matters*: Employers often face competing priorities, so a delayed response is rarely a sign of disinterest. Your balanced follow-up shows commitment while allowing them the opportunity to manage decisions on their timeline. This balance reflects professional maturity and conveys that you can engage with process without losing momentum.

5.4 Stay Persistent, Stay Prepared

Finding the job that feels like the perfect fit can take time, but persistence combined with preparation makes the process more sustainable. This section focuses on how to navigate the waiting periods productively, so that your progress is not defined only by whether an offer is in front of you. By approaching the search as an ongoing practice, you strengthen habits that extend beyond any single application: maintaining momentum through consistent effort, broadening your professional relationships with a focus on mutual value, and continuing to build skills that reinforce your long-term direction. Rather than measuring progress only by outcomes, you can use delays to treat preparation as an ongoing discipline; it strengthens judgment and ensures you approach the right opportunity with depth behind your readiness.

Don't Pause Your Progress: Even after a strong interview, it's important to keep your search active. Confidence in one opportunity can feel reassuring, yet the hiring process is shaped by factors outside your control. Continuing your efforts ensures that your options expand rather than narrow, which positions you to evaluate opportunities with a broader perspective through greater choice.

- *What to Do*: Keep applying for roles so your search stays active, but think of each application as part of a learning process rather than a race. Revisit your resume and cover letter with each new opportunity, using what you've learned from past interviews to make small adjustments. Stay connected to your field through professional groups, industry events, or online platforms where current trends are discussed. These steps help you stay connected to opportunities while also deepening your understanding of what different employers value.

- *Why It Matters*: Remaining engaged in your search ensures that you continue learning about employer expectations. Each role you pursue deepens your understanding of how your skills align with different opportunities, which makes your eventual decisions more informed. Remember, keeping your search active ensures your progress is defined by continued growth rather than the outcome of any single interview.

Expand Your Reach, Strengthen Your Skills: The time after an interview is an opportunity to stay engaged in your career path while building momentum for future opportunities. Investing in yourself during this stage helps you build continuity in your development, regardless of hiring timelines.

- *What to Do*: Start by joining industry groups and participating in networking activities. If you enjoy bigger events, attend conferences or expos. If you prefer smaller settings, webinars or one-on-one virtual coffee chats can be a good fit. At the same time, enhance your skills through online courses, certifications, or personal projects, especially those related to the feedback you received during your interviews.

- *Why It Matters*: Expanding your network makes a difference because it gives you access to how people in your field actually navigate opportunities, which helps you see patterns in what organizations look for. Developing your skills shows that growth is continuing on your terms, leaving you better positioned to engage when future opportunities become available.

5.5 Turning Setbacks into Wins

Hearing "no" is disappointing, but it need not diminish the work you've invested. Every rejection reinforces the resilience required to continue, reminding you that perseverance itself is part of professional growth. When viewed this way, a "no" becomes feedback that strengthens your preparation for future opportunities. Remember, progress is measured by what you learn along the way, not only by the offers you receive.

From Setback to Comeback: Rejection is rarely a judgment of your entire ability; more often, it reflects timing, organizational needs, or fit with the role. Recognizing this perspective helps you see each "no" as useful information rather than a fixed judgment.

- *What to Do*: After each rejection, take time to reflect on what the experience indicated about your approach. Look for recurring themes in feedback or outcomes, and use those insights to refine how you present yourself. Revisit your goals during this stage to confirm they reflect both your values and the direction you want your career path to take. This process ensures that each setback contributes to progress rather than standing as an endpoint.

- *Why It Matters*: Treating rejection as feedback positions it as part of the development process rather than as a disruption. Each experience adds to an understanding of how employers make decisions, offering insight into what to emphasize and how to prepare. Over time, these insights deepen understanding in evaluating opportunities, making development a product of reflection as much as achievement.

Strategic Use of Rejection: Thinking strategically about rejection means asking what the decision tells you about fit, expectations, and preparation. Framed this way, even a "no" can contribute to your progress.

- *What to Do*: When a role does not result in an offer, consider reaching out respectfully to ask for feedback. To make it easier to ask for feedback after a decision is made, see Toolkit 3: Feedback Request Template. Even brief comments can point to patterns in how employers view your qualifications or presentation, giving you focus areas for growth. Use these insights to adjust your resume, interview approach, or skill development in ways that reflect both your strengths and the expectations of your field. By applying feedback in this targeted way, each application builds on the last, creating continuous progress rather than repeating the same approach.

- *Why It Matters*: Rejection reflects more than a single outcome; it provides context about how decisions are made. Paying attention to those decisions adds to an understanding of what employers prioritize, which makes preparation more deliberate. Over time, this perspective helps progress feel continuous rather than interrupted by setbacks.

5.6 Wrap-Up: The Interview Follow-Up Playbook

The period after an interview is often overlooked, yet it contains feedback that can be turned into preparation. How you respond to outcomes; through follow-ups, reflection, and the use of feedback; influences how future opportunities are understood. This chapter has shown how to treat that stage as part of development rather than as a gap in the process. The following review highlights the key lessons from this chapter.

Key Takeaways

Section 5.1: The Immediate Follow-Up

- *Gratitude and Growth*: A thank-you email acknowledges the time and consideration offered by interviewers, while also reinforcing professionalism in how you finish the discussion on a respectful note. Over time, this practice shapes a reputation built on respect as much as ability.

- *Review and Refine*: Taking time to review an interview allows you to view it as part of a broader process rather than a single event. Noticing patterns in your interview provides perspective on both strengths and limits, turning reflection into actionable steps for preparation in upcoming opportunities.

Section 5.2: Growth Through Feedback

- *Feedback Fuels Progress*: Feedback bridges the gap between how you intended to present yourself and the impression it created with employers. Recognizing that difference shows where adjustments will have the greatest impact. This process strengthens judgment about both communication and preparation.

- *Implementing Feedback*: Applying feedback turns general advice into specific refinements that can be measured over time. Each change shows whether preparation is becoming more effective or if further refinement is needed. This approach deepens understanding of what consistently improves performance across opportunities.

Section 5.3: The Follow-Up Formula

- *Smart Follow-Up Moves*: A timely follow-up acknowledges the effort that went into the interview and confirms that you continue to value the opportunity. It turns the conversation into a complete exchange rather than a one-sided interaction. Over time, this practice strengthens the impression that you take opportunities seriously while respecting process.

- *When Silence is Loud*: Silence in the hiring process does not always indicate disinterest; it often reflects competing priorities within the organization. A well-timed follow-up reinforces engagement without placing pressure on the decision process. Patience expressed this way becomes part of the impression you leave with employers.

Section 5.4: Evolving Through Interviews

- *Build Confidence, Build Growth*: Treating each interview as part of development makes every experience valuable, regardless of the outcome. Reflection identifies decisions that strengthen how you present yourself as well as habits that may weaken your presentation. This approach builds adaptability while ensuring that progress is defined by learning as well as results.

Section 5.5: Stay Persistent, Stay Prepared

- *From Setback to Comeback*: Staying active in your search ensures that every interview contributes to preparation rather than serving as an endpoint. Applying to new roles gives you the chance to test how adjustments are received across different contexts. This approach reveals patterns in how employers interpret your qualifications.

- *Strategic Use of Rejection*: Not every opportunity leads to the outcome you hoped for, yet the time between interviews can still serve a purpose. Using rejection as a point to improve specific skills or expand professional relationships ensures the process continues to build value. This perspective keeps rejection tied to development rather than to disappointment.

Every interview, follow-up, or rejection provides more than a simple outcome; it creates a record of how preparation, communication, and decision-making are perceived in a professional setting. When each stage is treated as feedback, it leads to a better understanding of which aspects of preparation are effective and which approaches require adjustment. Viewed in this way, the focus shifts from single outcomes to the patterns that reveal how certain approaches consistently produce stronger results. It also leads naturally into the closing chapter, where the focus shifts to connecting these lessons with a wider view of motivation, perspective, and future choices.

"Resilience is knowing that you are the only one that has the power and the responsibility to pick yourself up." –
Mary Holloway

Chapter Six

Bringing It All Together

"When you find your why, you find a way to make it happen." - Eric Thomas

6.1 Exploring Your *Why*

The deeper value of an interview is found in the perspective it offers on alignment between personal motivation and professional direction. Beyond answering questions, it provides a setting to take a look at the reasons behind specific goals and choices. Approached in this way, preparation becomes a way of testing how well goals align with motivation: it becomes an opportunity to identify which goals are worth pursuing, why certain roles hold interest, and identify environments where consistent progress feels natural, not forced. This perspective links immediate performance to broader reflection, helping to ensure that professional choices grow out of personal motivation rather than the immediate demands of the hiring process.

Understanding Your Path: Interviews show how past choices, new skills, and evolving interests connect into a career path. Paying attention to this connection turns preparation into an opportunity to connect with deeper self-understanding.

- *What to Do*: Use interview preparation as a time to look at the strengths that interviewers have acknowledged more than once. Think about the skills you've developed through recent experiences and how they have influenced the kinds of roles you now find most rewarding. Review both the feedback provided by interviewers and the observations you've made after each conversation. Together they call attention to the settings where your approach creates the strongest impact and where adjustments could increase the range of roles available.

- *Why It Matters*: When preparation includes reflection, interviews become part of a larger learning process. They show which abilities remain consistent in different contexts, where growth would expand available opportunities, and the ways career interests evolve as responsibilities change. This perspective keeps career decisions tied to insight rather than to chance.

Learn as You Go: Interviews often teach as much as they test. The lessons they provide about strengths, limitations, and the direction those insights suggest can influence both preparation and whether a potential role fits both current strengths and future direction.

- *What to Do*: Interviews can be used to see how preparation carries into conversation. Attention to recurring questions shows where employers seek more depth. Reviewing whether examples connected to role requirements or left uncertainty highlights areas of strength as well as those that need adjustment. Remember, the value of an interview is not limited to the result; its contribution is the insight it provides into preparation, performance, and direction.

- *Why It Matters*: When interviews are viewed as opportunities for reflection, they provide insight into how preparation connects with performance. Over time, these observations make it easier to see patterns in strengths, recognize limits that need attention, and identify the kinds of roles where those strengths are best applied.

6.2 Mindset Matters

The role of mindset in a job search is often underestimated. Skills and preparation are important, but without a balanced perspective they can be undermined by frustration, impatience, or doubt. Viewing challenges through the lens of learning keeps the process from being defined only by immediate outcomes. Instead, each experience contributes to a more complete view of strengths, limits, and opportunities, supporting decisions that remain consistent with long-term priorities.

Positive Thinking, Positive Results: Mindset influences more than how the job search is experienced; it determines how outcomes are interpreted and how choices are made afterward. When results are seen as information rather than fixed results, even setbacks play a role in direction.

- ***What to Do***: Treat interviews as connected rather than isolated. Reflection on one conversation can influence the approach to the next, helping to build continuity rather than starting fresh each time. Continuity gives the search a sense of connection, where each experience adds perspective that strengthens the next.

- ***Why It Matters***: Continuity makes progress easier to track, since adjustments in preparation can be compared across interviews. It also reduces the pressure placed on any single outcome by showing that learning adds up, even when the result is disappointing.

Rising Above Challenges: A job search often involves periods of uncertainty, delayed responses, or outcomes that fall short of expectations. Resilience and persistence give those moments meaning, turning them into points of learning rather than reasons to stop.

- *What to Do*: When facing a setback, focus on setting small, achievable goals that keep your momentum going. Don't hesitate to reach out to your network for advice or encouragement, and always remind yourself of the progress you've made so far, no matter how small it might seem.

- *Why It Matters*: Without resilience and persistence, single outcomes risk being overvalued. These qualities keep setbacks within context, allowing growth to be understood across multiple experiences rather than defined by one result.

6.3 Looking Beyond the Now

Securing an interview is an achievement, but it should be viewed as a step in an ongoing process of development. Each conversation provides perspective not only on immediate opportunities but also on how choices today influence long-term direction. This section explores how to connect short-term actions with future priorities, including the kinds of professional relationships and goals that support direction beyond immediate roles.

Future-Focused Career Strategy: Strategic thinking about a career is not about predicting the future but about recognizing how current choices influence the opportunities that open up later. This perspective invites a deeper look at how interviews, job transitions, and ongoing learning combine to shape longer-term direction.

- *What to Do*: Develop goals by building them on lessons drawn from past experiences: consider which responsibilities felt most aligned with strengths, which skills drew recognition, and which environments supported growth. Review these goals at regular intervals, not only to check progress but to assess whether changing interests or external trends suggest a need for adjustment. When pursuing learning, identify gaps that limit advancement and select methods that directly address them, whether through formal programs, targeted training, or deliberate self-study.

- *Why It Matters*: Strategic planning helps distinguish between choices made from growth, those driven by necessity, and those reflecting a shift in priorities. This clarity ensures that career progress is not defined solely by circumstance but shaped by deliberate reflection. Over time, this perspective makes career decisions easier to interpret as part of a connected process rather than as separate outcomes.

Expanding Your Professional Circle: Professional connections matter because they influence the information available, the perspectives considered, and the options that can realistically be pursued. Seen this way, relationships are not just helpful in finding roles but are part of how a career develops over time.

- *What to Do*: Engage with others in ways that create mutual value rather than one-sided conversations. Look for forums such as professional groups, educational settings, or informal discussions that connect you to perspectives you wouldn't find alone. When building connections, focus on mutual benefit by offering insight or assistance where possible while remaining open to learning from the experience of others. With consistency, professional circles highlight patterns in advice, opportunities, and expectations that connect individual steps to a wider context of professional expectations. Remember, a professional circle is not a substitute for preparation, but it can strengthen the decisions that preparation supports.

- *Why It Matters*: The strength of a network lies not only in opportunity but in perspective. This perspective allows progress to be interpreted against professional standards rather than personal expectations alone.

6.4 The Bigger Picture

Careers are often described in terms of advancement, but they are better understood through the motivations that explain why certain directions were chosen. Looking at choices in this way emphasizes the values, interests, and commitments that continue to influence decisions across different roles and environments. This section explores how recognizing those underlying patterns positions career planning as a way to build continuity, linking current opportunities with longer-term direction. It places emphasis on the reasoning behind choices, making career progress more intentional and less reactive.

Realize Your Potential: Strengths are not abstract qualities but abilities proven through experience. By recognizing where strengths have consistently reinforced growth, it becomes easier to judge whether new roles will extend development or risk weakening momentum.

- *What to Do*: Take a look at the situations where your involvement changed the direction of the outcome. Ask not only what you did, but why it worked: was it problem-solving, persistence in the face of setbacks, or coordination that aligned others toward a shared goal? Strengths become more dependable markers of growth when they influence results in both routine and high-stakes situations. This perspective turns experience into a more balanced reference point for considering new opportunities.

- *Why It Matters*: Strengths that have proven effective in different contexts provide more than confidence for an interview; they serve as benchmarks for evaluating future opportunities. This perspective makes long-term planning less speculative and more firmly based on experience.

Finding Purpose in Your Career: Career decisions often rely on assumptions about what will work in the future, yet interviews offer examples of where abilities have reinforced growth across different contexts. Recognizing recurring strengths gives perspective on which opportunities extend proven abilities and which may leave them underutilized.

- *What to Do*: Take a look at situations where the outcome depended on your involvement. Ask why your contribution mattered: was it critical thinking that identified the root of an issue, follow-through that ensured commitments were met, or relationship-building that strengthened cooperation? What counts as a strength is not a single achievement but an ability that has influenced results across both routine tasks and complex challenges. Remember, the role of a strength is to connect past contribution with future direction, offering continuity across change.

- *Why It Matters*: What makes recurring strengths important is their ability to support both communication and choice. In interviews, they reinforce more than potential by showing results already achieved, and in career planning, they act as benchmarks for deciding where future growth is most likely.

6.5 Your Next Move

You've worked through ideas that reframe how interviews are prepared for and how opportunities are evaluated. The value of those ideas expands when they move from reflection into goals that define priorities and support intentional progress. In this section, the focus turns to setting goals that connect preparation with outcomes, providing a way to compare effort against results and identify methods that are worth repeating.

Purposeful Goals, Powerful Outcomes: A job search without goals often feels like movement without direction. Goals provide a way to measure what has been effective, point to areas needing further attention, and ensure that preparation produces knowledge that can be applied to career choices ahead.

- *What to Do*: Set goals that create information you can use. Track whether applications tailored to specific roles receive stronger responses, whether networking conversations lead to meaningful follow-up, or whether interview practice shows clearer differentiation between skills, strengths, and outcomes. Interpreting these results creates accountability, showing whether the time invested in preparation is producing results that justify continuing the same approach. The analysis shows whether preparation is reinforcing abilities employers recognize, ensuring time spent contributes to credibility as well as readiness.

- *Why It Matters*: By linking preparation to proven abilities, career development becomes more intentional. Progress can be evaluated through patterns of what has worked rather than one-off achievements or disappointments. It provides assurance that development is not accidental but reinforced by abilities that have proven their value.

Stepping into Your Future: Progress begins when insight influences behavior. What you decide to do now, whether refining a skill, seeking feedback, or taking on challenges that advance your professional maturity, becomes a measure of how your abilities are developing.

- *What to Do*: Define the standards that reflect personal values and professional direction, such as how a role contributes to sustained professional growth, whether it makes full use of existing abilities, and whether it supports long-term priorities. Use these standards as consistent benchmarks when considering opportunities so decisions rest on more than immediate circumstance. At the same time, revisit two recent accomplishments and reframe them to emphasize both the skills applied and the outcomes achieved. The dual focus provides both a method for considering opportunities and a language for explaining professional advancement.

- *Why It Matters*: Standards provide a safeguard against reactive choices that may undermine growth. Reinforced by outcomes already achieved, they ensure progress is driven by standards that translate into measurable progress, showing a clear link between past performance and future potential.

6.6 Wrap-Up: Closing the Deal

Ending here offers a chance to reframe how progress is understood. Growth is not a single evolution but an accumulation of standards applied, lessons integrated, and actions tested over time. The value of this book rests in how its ideas redefine the questions asked, the benchmarks applied, and the meaning assigned to success. Remember, the standards chosen for decisions will define the course of a career more than any external outcome.

Key Takeaways

Section 6.1: Exploring Your *Why*

- ***Understanding Your Path***: Treat the interview process as more than a test of qualifications. It is a structured setting that shows how priorities align with available opportunities. By asking questions and reflecting on the answers, it becomes possible to see whether a role supports long-term direction, fits with personal values, and advances professional development. Used this way, interviews are not just about selection but about building clarity in decision-making.

- ***Learn As You Go***: Every interview functions as more than an evaluation; it is a learning opportunity. The process shows which skills draw the strongest connection to the employer's needs, how well priorities are understood, and where adjustments may be necessary to better align with professional goals.

Section 6.2: Mindset Matters

- ***Positive Thinking, Positive Results***: Maintaining perspective in the job search keeps attention on what can be controlled, such as preparation, communication, and follow-up, instead of allowing results to overshadow the process.

- *Rising Above Challenges*: Breaking challenges into smaller components creates clarity. Some parts can be addressed immediately,
  some require additional preparation, and others may depend on outside factors. Separating challenges this way prevents wasted energy
  and directs effort toward the areas where progress is possible.

Section 6.3: Looking Beyond the Now

- *Future-Focused Career Strategy*: Treat each career decision as part
  of a larger plan. Interviews, role changes, and professional commitments should be evaluated not only for their immediate benefits but
  for how they build toward the skills, responsibilities, and outcomes
  that prepare you for greater responsibility.

- *Expanding Your Professional Circle*: Building relationships in your
  field is more than collecting names. The people you connect with
  can share insight into how the work is done, provide perspective
  on career choices, and open doors to opportunities that may not be
  visible otherwise.

Section 6.4: The Bigger Picture

- *Realize Your Potential*: Potential is not abstract; it is shown through the situations where actions change results. That may mean leading a process that reduced errors, developing a solution that others adopted, or contributing an approach that improved performance across a team. Recognizing these recurring points of influence turns isolated experiences into a record of distinction that can guide future choices.

- *Finding Purpose in Your Career*: Career decisions take on greater importance when they reflect personal values. Work reinforced by a strong connection to personal values builds consistency, reduces the risk of burnout, and encourages connections with peers who recognize and respect those priorities.

Section 6.5: Your Next Move

- *Purposeful Goals, Powerful Outcomes*: When you break your job search into tangible steps, like setting aside hours for networking or a target number of applications, you create a personal roadmap that makes the journey less intimidating. This creates a roadmap that makes the journey less overwhelming and boosts your confidence by giving you control over the process.

- ***Move with Intention***: Each step you take; whether revising your resume or reaching out to new contacts; becomes more consistent with where you want to go when it reflects your ambitions and career goals. This structured approach shifts the search from a series of tasks into a direction shaped by intention, creating momentum toward roles that reinforce the career path you want to follow.

6.7 Your Time to Shine

As this book reaches its conclusion, it becomes important to recognize the commitment that has sustained progress throughout these chapters. Progress here has not been passive; it has been strengthened through consistent effort, careful reflection, and the willingness to sit with ideas until their value became clear. Each section has required effort, and that effort has already strengthened the ability to approach challenges with a focus on process rather than immediate outcomes. What now exists is a framework for decision-making that reflects both the effort invested and the insights gained along the way. What has been established will grow with experience, adapting to the varied demands of future challenges. Remember, the value of this work lies in its ability to influence the choices that follow, not in the fact that it has been completed.

- *Believe in Yourself*: Belief in one's abilities comes from recognizing the persistence it has taken to reach this stage. Every challenge faced, every lesson drawn from setbacks, and every success earned has created strengths that show the difference between what was learned in theory and what was lived in practice. Employers notice the persistence shown in completing difficult work, not just the title that was held.

- *Adapt and Innovate*: Change is not a disruption but a constant part of professional life. Every piece of feedback offers direction, and each new experience shows whether that direction leads to improvement. These repeated adjustments form a pattern that establishes the capacity to learn in motion. Employers notice this, because it reflects the reality of modern workplaces where flexibility is as important as technical expertise.

- *Stay Resilient*: Difficulty is not a sign of failure but a natural part of growth. Every challenge encountered offers a reminder that persistence matters as much as ability. Continuing through periods of difficulty shows that progress is not erased by setbacks but strengthened through them. Employers notice resilience because it shows that responsibility is taken seriously, even when setbacks occur.

- *Celebrate Every Milestone*: Progress develops through steady progression, and each achievement reinforces habits that prepare you for larger responsibilities. Landing an interview, receiving positive feedback, or refining your resume add to the professional track record you are building, and they prove that consistent effort translates into career momentum.

- *Leverage Your Resources*: Progress is easier when you benefit from the experience of others. Mentors, peers, and professional communities provide insights that shorten the learning curve and provide direction on actions that improve outcomes. Making use of these connections ensures you're not relying solely on trial and error.

- ***Progress Through Practice***: Each interview reinforces skills needed for future responsibilities. These experiences refine communication, decision-making, and problem-solving abilities, establishing patterns of performance employers recognize. The process gradually shifts what once felt difficult into what now feels manageable.

- ***Look Back at Your Progress***: Taking the time to look back shows more than a record of past choices; it highlights patterns of growth, strategies that have proven effective, and areas that would benefit from more practice. Reflection turns experiences into lessons, helping to highlight where past choices have led to the strongest results. Remember, the strongest guide for tomorrow often comes from the experiences of yesterday.

In closing, the insights established throughout these chapters do not stand apart from daily life; they provide a framework for approaching decisions with consistency. Each lesson adds to a pattern that shows how persistence, reflection, and adaptation create momentum that extends into every stage of professional growth. Progress will continue to take shape through this process, giving weight to every decision that follows.

"The only person you are destined to become is the person you decide to be" - Ralph Waldo Emerson

Toolkit 1: Personal Pitch Workshop

Introduction: A personal pitch is often the first time someone hears your story in your own words. Done well, it shows not only what you've achieved but also how you think and what you value. This toolkit gives you the structure to share that story in a way that feels natural while ensuring others walk away with a clear sense of your potential.

Step 1: Reflect on What Makes You, *You*

Your Skills and Strengths: Start by writing a list of your top skills and strengths.

- *When people describe your contributions, what qualities do they mention?*

- *How have your skills supported progress in school, work, or personal growth?*

- *How does your presence, mindset, or approach tend to make work easier or more effective for others?*

- **Remember:** Each achievement tells a story about how you work, what you value, and the determination you bring to reaching your goals.

Your Professional Experiences: Think about the roles, projects, or challenges that have had the biggest impact on your career path:

- *Which experiences required you to rethink your usual approach to reach a goal, and how did those adjustments influence how you work today?*

- *What did you learn about the environments that bring out your best work: team settings, independent work, fast-paced environments, or structured systems?*

- *How did those experiences influence what you expect of yourself in a professional setting?*

- **Reflection Point:** The experiences that influence our direction most often happen quietly; they shift how we think, decide, or approach our work long before others notice the change.

Your Achievements: Write down the achievements that gave you a sense of progress or validation in your work:

- *How do these successes reflect the areas where you've consistently performed well?*

- *How have these experiences influenced the way you approach new challenges?*

- *How have those experiences influenced the way you decide what's worth pursuing today?*

- **Remember:** Every accomplishment tells part of your story. The real insight comes from recognizing what each one says about your persistence, focus, and willingness to keep improving.

Step 2: Create Your Story

Career Milestones: Outline the major milestones in your career so far:

- *Looking back, how did each experience influence the direction you chose to pursue next?*

- *What patterns do you notice between the opportunities you pursued and the ones that felt most rewarding?*

- *How do the steps you've taken so far influence the direction you're considering now?*

- **Insight:** A pitch feels stronger when others can follow the reasoning behind your choices. Showing how each step built on what came before helps people see consistency in how you approach growth.

Challenges Overcome: Think about a major challenge you've faced:

- *How did it test your ability to adapt, collaborate, or lead?*

- *What strengths became more visible when you were pushed outside your usual comfort zone?*

- *How did that experience influence the kind of risks you're now willing to take?*

- **Tip**: The way you handle challenges often tells employers more about your mindset and decision-making than any list of accomplishments could.

Why You're Unique: Consider the skills and decisions that set your career apart from others:

- *How does your background give you a perspective that others may not have?*

- *Which experiences have helped you see the connection between what you value and how you contribute?*

- *How have you earned the trust of peers, leaders, or clients in past experiences?*

- **Reflection:** Your uniqueness is often a blend of mindset, consistency, and curiosity: qualities that continue to strengthen your professional value no matter where your path leads.

Step 3: Connect Your Strengths to Employer Needs

Understanding the Role and Company: Get a sense of what the company values and what this role is meant to improve.

- *What do recent initiatives or job descriptions tell you about their direction?*

- *Which of your experiences best show you can strengthen results for people, processes, or performance?*

- *How might your perspective help them think differently about a challenge they face?*

- **Tip:** The goal isn't to fit into their culture; it's to show how your contribution would enhance it.

Design Your Pitch: Connect your experience to their goals:

- *Which examples best reflect your understanding of the work, the expectations, and the impact of the role?*

- *How can you connect your language to the organization's tone: formal, collaborative, or innovative, while keeping your delivery consistent with who you are?*

- *What's one story you could share that reflects the way your approach contributed to stronger performance, efficiency, or morale?*

- **Remember**: A strong pitch doesn't just tell them who you are; it helps them see you in the role.

Step 4: Practice Your Delivery

Practicing How You Speak About Yourself: Rehearse a 1–2 minute version of your story that feels conversational without sounding rehearsed.

- Focus on flow, not memorization.

- Say it out loud to ensure it sounds natural, not scripted.

- Share your pitch with a friend or peer who doesn't know your full background; see if they can summarize your main strengths after hearing it once.

- *Tip: Focus on conversation, not delivery. You're sharing insight, not giving a speech.*

Feedback and Refinement: Gather perspective from people who can see both your strengths and blind spots.

- Invite feedback on what people found most memorable; those responses help you understand how your message connects with others.

- Think about whether the feedback reflects the image and strengths you're intentionally working to communicate.

- Find the balance between being consistent with who you are and being prepared; your delivery should sound confident without sounding rehearsed.

- ***Reflection:*** *Refinement isn't about changing your message; it's about deepening your connection to it so others experience it as authentically as you intend.*

Step 5: Prepare for Questions

Anticipating Follow-Up Questions: Think ahead about the kinds of questions an interviewer might ask:

- What parts of your story make others want to know more about your experiences or decisions?

- How might your responses show how you think through situations, adjust when plans change, and stay aligned with what's important to you?

- Which examples help others see not just what you did, but how you approached decisions, handled setbacks, or learned from outcomes?

- *Tip: A good follow-up answer feels like a continuation of your story; not a defense of it.*

Final Thoughts

Your personal pitch will continue to evolve as you do. Every new project, challenge, or accomplishment adds perspective to how you describe what you offer. Revisiting your pitch regularly helps you stay connected to that growth and ensures what you share still reflects where you are and where you're headed. Try reviewing it a few times each year to capture what has changed. Over time, you'll notice that your story becomes less about what you've done and more about who you've become through those experiences.

Toolkit 2: Questions That Strengthen Your Perspective

Introduction: Your questions help establish the level of understanding between you and the interviewer just as much as your answers do. They allow you to assess whether the company's culture, leadership style, and expectations support the kind of work environment you want to be part of. You'll find examples designed to deepen your understanding of the company, its environment, and how you might contribute within it.

Decision-Making Process

- *What to Ask*: *"How are decisions made in the team? Is it a collaborative process?"*

- *Why it Matters*: Decision-making is one of the most telling aspects of a company's culture. A collaborative model suggests an environment that values shared insight, learning, and growth through dialogue. A hierarchical approach, while efficient, might focus more on execution than exploration. Recognizing which model a company follows helps you anticipate how much space there is for creativity, initiative, and learning from others.

Feedback Culture

- *What to Ask*: *"What does the feedback process look like here, is it ongoing or tied mainly to performance reviews?"*

- *Why It Matters*: Feedback shapes how people grow, learn, and stay engaged. A healthy feedback culture creates mutual trust, where guidance is viewed as support rather than criticism. Understanding how feedback is exchanged helps you see whether the organization invests in developing people or simply evaluating performance. Balanced feedback offers direction, helping you understand both what's working and where growth can continue.

Long-Term Development

- ***What to Ask***: *"How have others in this role transitioned into new challenges or leadership opportunities?"*

- ***Why It Matters***: This question clarifies whether the company views professional growth as a shared responsibility or an individual pursuit. When development is treated as a partnership between employees and leaders, employees often experience a deeper connection to their work. When growth depends largely on personal initiative, the pace and visibility of progress may vary. Recognizing that balance helps you plan how to approach your own advancement.

Understanding How Success Is Defined

- ***What to Ask***: *"How is success typically measured for someone in this role?"*

- ***Why It Matters***: How a company measures results reveals where it places the most importance; consistency, innovation, collaboration, or independence. These priorities influence how decisions are made, how achievements are recognized, and how responsibility is balanced between individuals and leadership. Understanding them helps you assess whether your strengths align with what the company recognizes and rewards.

Team Dynamics

- ***What to Ask***: *"What are the biggest strengths of this team? What challenges does it face?"*

- ***Why It Matters***: A team's strengths often reveal its identity; what it values, how it collaborates, and what drives results. Asking about both strengths and challenges gives you a realistic view of the environment you may join. It helps you understand where your abilities could reinforce success and where adaptability might be needed. This awareness allows you to prepare for how you'd position your strengths to support the team's direction.

Onboarding and Training Process

- ***What to Ask***: *"Can you walk me through what the onboarding experience typically looks like for someone in this role?"*

- ***Why It Matters***: The way a company approaches onboarding reflects how it views people: as investments to be developed or resources to be used. Every decision in that process, from communication style to timing, sends subtle cues about transparency, support, and respect for learning. These patterns often mirror how leadership handles development at every stage, giving you a preview of what long-term experience in the organization might feel like.

Client or Customer Interaction

- *What to Ask*: *"How frequently does this role engage with clients or customers, and in what ways?"*

- *Why It Matters*: The way a role engages with clients or customers reflects how the organization defines partnership: transactional or relationship-driven. Every exchange, from tone to follow-through, reflects how consistently the organization applies its stated values in real interactions. These patterns often offer insight into how leadership views connection: as a strategic advantage or as an obligation that ends once expectations are met.

Leadership Development

- *What to Ask*: *"What opportunities are there for leadership development within the company?"*

- *Why It Matters*: The way a company approaches leadership development reflects how it views growth: as a shared responsibility or a personal pursuit. The structure, accessibility, and consistency of these opportunities offer insight into whether learning is treated as an ongoing priority or an optional benefit. This helps you gauge whether the organization builds a culture that develops leaders from within or relies on individual initiative to fill future roles.

Understanding the Organization

- **What to Ask**: *"Who does this department collaborate with most often, and what does that collaboration usually look like?"*

- **Why It Matters**: The way an organization is structured conveys what leadership values most: efficiency, innovation, or control. The flow of information and decision-making shows whether access to leadership and collaboration is encouraged or filtered through layers of approval. Understanding these relationships helps you assess whether the structure aligns with how you work best: through collaboration, autonomy, or direct access to decision-makers.

Role Status

- **What to Ask**: *"Is this a newly created role, or will I be stepping into an existing position?"*

- **Why It Matters**: Knowing whether a position is new or previously held gives you perspective on how prepared the organization is to support a new person entering the role. A new position may come with freedom to influence priorities but also fewer examples to follow. A replacement role can provide structure yet still carry expectations shaped by someone else's approach. Understanding this helps you anticipate the level of guidance, patience, and learning you'll need as you settle into the role.

Remote Work Policies

- **What to Ask**: *"How does the company support remote employees in terms of resources, training, and career development opportunities?"*

- **Why It Matters**: The way a company supports remote employees shows how seriously leadership treats inclusion when people aren't physically present. A well-structured system provides access to communication channels, leadership visibility, and development opportunities equal to those in the office. Understanding this helps you judge whether you'll be recognized for your work or need to compete for attention from a distance: a difference that can define both performance and growth.

Employee Success Stories

- **What to Ask**: *"Could you share a recent success story of an employee in this department?"*

- **Why It Matters**: Employee success stories reflect how recognition is built into the culture. What leaders choose to highlight, whether team effort, innovation, or perseverance, shows what's valued through everyday actions, not just in mission statements. Observing these examples helps you identify how the company aligns its values with its actions, and whether success feels shared or individual within the environment you'd join.

Cross-Functional Project Opportunities

- *What to Ask*: *"Are there opportunities to work on projects with teams from different departments?"*

- *Why It Matters*: How departments work together shows how information moves through the organization and how connected leadership really is. Cross-functional projects indicate whether collaboration is built into daily operations or happens only when goals temporarily align. Understanding this helps you gauge how decisions are made, how feedback is shared, and whether the environment supports shared problem-solving or reinforces silos.

Professional Development Funding

- *What to Ask*: *"Does the company offer financial support for professional development activities, such as workshops, membership in professional associations, or certifications?"*

- *Why It Matters*: How a company approaches professional development funding offers insight into whether leadership sees learning as a one-time benefit or a continuous investment. An ongoing commitment to training and education shows that growth isn't viewed as an afterthought but as part of how the organization ensures its capacity to evolve. Observing how funding decisions are made gives you a sense of whether leadership plans for sustained growth or treats development as a short-term measure rather than an ongoing responsibility.

Mentorship Programs

- *What to Ask*: "Does the company have a formal mentorship program?"

- *Why It Matters*: A formal mentorship program shows whether leadership builds learning into the organization's structure or relies on it to occur informally. When development is supported by structured mentorship, it shows that leadership values continuity: the transfer of knowledge, perspective, and accountability across experience levels. Understanding how mentorship is supported helps you see whether growth is treated as an ongoing responsibility supported by leadership or as something employees are expected to navigate on their own.

Approach to Work-Life Balance

- *What to Ask*: "How does the company support employees in maintaining a healthy work-life balance?"

- *Why It Matters*: Work-life balance reflects how mature leadership is in understanding the connection between well-being and sustained performance. The credibility of that belief is shown in how leaders handle urgency, boundaries, and recovery time. Understanding how these dynamics are managed gives you insight into whether you'll be encouraged to maintain balance or expected to sacrifice it when priorities compete.

Toolkit 3: Silent Signals in Interviews

Introduction: Long before the first question, employers begin forming an impression. They notice how you walk in, take your seat, or respond to introductions. Those early observations can influence how your answers are received through the remainder of the interview. This toolkit helps you understand how your non-verbal communication shapes perception and gives you ways to project a sense of ease, focus, and professionalism throughout the interview.

Eye Contact

- *Message*: Communicates focus, sincerity, and readiness to engage.

- *Why It Matters*: In interviews, people often remember how connected they felt during the conversation. Eye contact helps build that connection. It shows that you're attentive to what's being said and that you value the exchange itself, not just the outcome.

Smiling

- *Message*: Communicates openness, composure, and warmth.

- *Why It Matters*: A smile conveys perspective. It shows that you recognize the interview as a shared conversation rather than a test. That mindset helps you stay grounded, reflecting confidence that comes from self-awareness rather than control.

Posture

- *Message*: Communicates composure, balance, and self-awareness.

- *Why It Matters*: Posture reflects how you manage the moment when the focus shifts to you. It's less about sitting straight and more about showing you're comfortable being seen. That balance of ease and attentiveness communicates quiet confidence without needing to assert it.

Nodding

- *Message*: Communicates patience, awareness, and engagement.

- *Why It Matters*: Nodding shows that you're processing what's being said, not just hearing it. It reflects respect for the other person's perspective while showing patience in how you respond. That awareness creates rhythm in conversation, allowing both sides to feel understood without interruption.

Hand Gestures

- *Message*: Communicates confidence through measured expression.

- *Why It Matters*: The way you use your hands reflects your relationship to the message. Controlled gestures suggest comfort with your ideas, while restless movement can imply uncertainty. Awareness of how you communicate through nonverbal expression reflects composure rooted in self-understanding.

Leaning In

- *Message*: Communicates interest guided by awareness and respect.

- *Why It Matters*: This subtle movement reflects how you participate in conversation without taking control of it. Leaning in conveys that you're invested in understanding the other person's perspective while remaining aware of the mutual respect being built. That awareness supports dialogue that feels collaborative rather than transactional.

Fidgeting

- *Message*: Communicates restlessness that draws attention away from your message.

- *Why It Matters*: Even subtle fidgeting can interrupt the flow of conversation. It suggests that attention is turned inward, toward discomfort, rather than outward, toward connection. Recognizing and redirecting that behavior allows you to remain engaged in the exchange rather than distracted by the pressure surrounding it.

Crossed Arms

- *Message*: Communicates guardedness or hesitation to engage.

- *Why It Matters*: Crossed arms affect how others experience your willingness to engage. In an interview, this posture can unintentionally reduce the sense of cooperation or trust that supports open, two-way communication. Becoming aware of this response allows you to show that you're comfortable with collaboration and confident handling perspectives different from your own.

Foot Tapping

- *Message*: Communicates a shift from engagement to self-regulation.

- *Why It Matters*: Foot tapping reflects a shift in focus from communication to internal regulation. It usually occurs when focus begins transitioning from processing information to managing internal tension. Recognizing that shift helps you slow your response, steady your posture, and bring attention back to the discussion rather than the discomfort.

Facial Expressions

- *Message*: Communicates engagement through expression.

- *Why It Matters*: Facial expressions reflect how engaged you are with the conversation. They offer subtle cues about how relaxed, attentive, and receptive you are to what's being shared. Awareness of your expressions helps connect what you intend to say with how it's interpreted, reducing chances of misunderstanding.

Firm Handshake

- *Message*: Communicates respect, readiness, and composure.

- *Why It Matters*: This brief exchange occurs before any questions are asked, giving interviewers an early reference for how you enter a professional conversation. That reference often becomes the baseline against which your engagement, tone, and responses are understood.

Checking the Time

- *Message*: Communicates divided focus between the conversation and external concerns.

- *Why It Matters*: When an interviewer notices you checking the time, they may assume your priorities are elsewhere. Even if unintentional, the gesture redirects attention from what's being discussed to how you're being perceived. Staying present communicates respect for shared time and awareness of how subtle actions influence perception.

Sighing

- *Message*: Communicates subtle disengagement.

- *Why It Matters*: A sigh may seem harmless, yet in a professional set-ting it can suggest that patience or interest has worn thin. It usually occurs when attention moves away from the discussion to the feeling of waiting. That shift indicates that frustration has replaced focus. In an interview, that small behavioral cue can make the conversation feel less collaborative and more transactional.

Head Tilting

- *Message*: Communicates engagement in what's being shared.

- *Why It Matters*: Head tilting during an interview reflects a willing-ness to connect rather than just listen. It usually occurs when interest shifts from absorbing what's being said to showing interest in the flow of the conversation. This small gesture shows a willingness to understand another perspective and reinforces that you're partici-pating, not just responding.

Breathing Rate

- *Message*: Communicates your level of composure under pressure.

- *Why It Matters*: Breathing influences more than composure; it regulates how clearly your mind processes information. When breathing becomes controlled, the body shifts out of its defensive state, allowing the mind to organize thoughts instead of racing through them. This sense of control helps you respond with balance between what you feel and what you want to say.

Voice Pitch

- *Message*: Communicates emotional regulation.

- *Why It Matters*: Interviewers often form impressions about your confidence from how your voice sounds. The human ear registers changes in pitch as changes in emotion, so even minor shifts can alter perceived credibility. Keeping tone within a natural range reinforces trust in both your message and your presence.

Toolkit 4: Post-Interview Analysis Template

Purpose: The *Post-Interview Analysis Template* helps you think through how your interview went and what you learned from it. Taking a few minutes to reflect after each interview gives you space to recognize what worked well, where you can adjust, and what each experience says about the kind of environment you want to be part of. Over time, these reflections become a collection of experiences that show your development, helping you approach each new opportunity with greater awareness and direction.

Create Your Document: Choose either a physical notebook or a digital document for recording your reflections after each interview. Organize it with the sections below, so it's easy to complete and review whenever you need. This process not only tracks progress but also deepens understanding; helping future preparation feel more intentional and grounded.

Personal Information

- *Date of Interview*:

- *Company Name*:

- *Position Applied For*:

- *Interview Format (Virtual, In-Person, Panel, etc.)*:

Interview Reflections

First Impressions

- *What observations did you make about the environment and tone of the interview?*

- *How did you feel before the conversation began, and how did that affect your focus?*

- *What did you notice about the interviewer's communication style or energy?*

Performance Assessment

- *Which responses felt strong or well-received, and why?*

- *Which questions challenged you? How did you manage them?*

- *Were your examples specific enough to show your experience clearly?*

- *Looking back, is there something you wish you had emphasized in greater detail?*

Engagement and Interaction

- *Did you stay engaged with the dialogue from start to finish?*

- *Did you stay engaged with what was being asked, or rely on what you had prepared?*

- *How balanced was the conversation between sharing information and building connection?*

- *What responses indicated the conversation felt mutual rather than one-sided?*

Company Culture and Role Fit

- *What insights did you gather about the company's values and decision-making style?*

- *How do their expectations align with how you like to work or grow?*

- *Did the environment feel supportive, structured, flexible, or competitive; and how does that align with your preferences?*

Learning and Growth

- *What did you notice about how you communicated; both in what you said and how you said it?*

- *Has this experience helped you define what you're looking for in your next role?*

- *What did you learn about how your strengths are perceived or understood by others?*

Feedback Received

- *Did the interviewer offer direct or indirect feedback about your experience, approach, or fit?*

- *What will you do differently next time based on what you learned here?*

- *If no feedback was given, what patterns in tone, pacing, or body language offer insight into how you came across?*

Next Steps and Actions

- *What are your immediate follow-up actions (thank-you email, LinkedIn connection, application tracking)?*

- *Based on this experience, what specific improvements will you focus on before your next interview?*

- *How will you keep your momentum going after this interview process? (e.g., setting weekly application goals or reflecting on interview takeaways before the next one)*

- *How soon do you expect to hear back, and what will you do if you don't?*

Additional Notes

- *Did the interview stand out as especially positive, surprising, or challenging?*

- *What themes or expectations appeared most important to the interviewer?*

- *What would you like to remember most from this experience?*

Using the Template: Complete the template soon after each interview, while your thoughts are still fresh. Review it regularly to:

- Assess trends in your interviews to understand where you're gaining traction or losing momentum.

- Compare how different companies make you feel about your potential fit.

- Refine how you prepare, answer questions, and evaluate opportunities.

- See how your self-awareness has enhanced the quality of your communication.

Review and Update: Revisit your collected reflections every few weeks or after several interviews. Look for:

- Stronger presence in how you interact, listen, and respond during interviews.

- Common themes in feedback that reveal growth opportunities.

- Changes in what you now look for in a work environment.

Through reflection, experience matures into understanding. Over time, that understanding becomes a foundation for evaluating new opportunities with patience, insight, and a stronger sense of direction. Remember: what you learn about yourself in the process often proves more valuable than any single result.

Toolkit 5: Job Offer Negotiation Strategies

Introduction: The moment a job offer arrives can bring excitement, relief, and a fair amount of uncertainty. You don't need to rush a decision or respond immediately when an offer arrives; taking time to reflect is both professional and expected. By approaching the conversation with a clear understanding of what you need and how to communicate it, you guide the discussion toward shared understanding that respects both your goals and the employer's position. Whether you're considering compensation, benefits, or long-term growth, this guide helps you make decisions that align with your values and professional direction.

Researching Industry Standards

Topic: Understanding compensation norms in your industry and specific role.

- *What to Do*: Review data from credible sources such as industry reports, salary comparison tools, and professional associations (e.g., U.S. Bureau of Labor Statistics, Glassdoor, PayScale). When possible, discuss compensation trends with trusted contacts who understand the market for your role and level of experience.

- *Why It Matters*: Awareness of compensation ranges strengthens your position and provides a factual basis for your requests. It reduces uncertainty, helping you engage in discussions that are informed rather than reactive. With this understanding, you can approach each offer as a data-driven decision rather than an emotional one, ensuring your choices reflect reasoning that balances value with opportunity.

Evaluating the Entire Offer

Topic: Considering all aspects of the job offer: salary, benefits, growth, and alignment with personal values.

- *What to Do*: Identify the aspects of the offer that influence your satisfaction and prioritize them before negotiation. Consider salary, healthcare, time off, flexibility, career development, and cultural fit as interrelated considerations that influence one another.

- *Why It Matters*: Looking at the offer in its entirety gives you insight into how compensation, culture, and growth connect. This broader view helps you evaluate what supports where you're headed professionally rather than what simply feels comfortable now. Decisions made from this understanding tend to support sustainable growth and greater satisfaction over time.

Articulating Your Value

Topic: Communicating impact through specific, outcome-based examples.

- *What to Do*: Reference specific examples of results you've achieved: process improvements, project outcomes, or measurable contributions to team success. Connect these examples to how you can add value in the new role.

- *Why It Matters*: When you describe the difference your work has made, you help the employer see how your experience connects to their needs. It shifts the discussion from compensation to contribution, reinforcing that what defines professional value is the difference you make, not the position you hold.

Preparing for the Negotiation Discussion

Topic: Developing a composed, professional communication style for negotiation.

- *What to Do*: Rehearse your approach with someone you trust who can offer candid feedback. Focus on how clearly you communicate your priorities, how well you explain your reasoning, and how calmly you respond to questions or challenges. Let each session help you understand your communication habits and strengthen how you express value.

- *Why It Matters*: Practice exposes how quickly emotion influences reason when the outcome carries personal significance. It gives you the distance to observe your own reactions: when you rush, defend, or over-explain, and to replace those impulses with reasoning that helps you respond to the person, not just the pressure. That awareness strengthens your ability to separate reaction from response, regardless of the situation.

Understanding When to Compromise

Topic: Setting clear priorities before negotiating.

- *What to Do:* Before any discussion, outline your priorities in order of importance. Differentiate between what directly supports your development and what caters to immediate interest. For example, you might accept a slightly lower salary if the role includes learning opportunities or exposure to projects that broaden your experience. Protect what drives long-term growth while staying open to flexibility in areas that create mutual value.

- *Why It Matters*: Defining your priorities brings structure to what can otherwise feel uncertain. It keeps the discussion focused on outcomes that reflect your goals rather than short-term benefits. When you understand the difference between what supports your development and what simply adds appeal, you negotiate from a place of good judgment. That insight helps you reach agreements that strengthen both your position and professional relationships.

Taking Time Before You Decide

Topic: Stepping back to consider each part of the offer.

- *What to Do*: Express appreciation for the offer and request a short review period, typically one to three days, to evaluate how the offer aligns with your priorities, responsibilities, and direction. Review the offer in context: how the role complements your experience, values, and career progression.

- *Why It Matters*: Reflection provides structure to decision-making, allowing you to evaluate an offer based on direction rather than emotion. When you take time to study what the role contributes to your growth, the details start to show whether it supports meaningful progress or temporary satisfaction. This shift turns the process of accepting a job into a way to recognize alignment between your goals and the environment that supports them.

Negotiating in Writing

Topic: Confirming the details of your job offer in writing.

- *What to Do:* After reaching a verbal agreement, request a revised offer letter that outlines every negotiated detail; salary, benefits, start date, and other commitments. Review it line by line to confirm consistency with your earlier communications. If any part differs from what was agreed, follow up directly to address the discrepancy before signing. Taking this step reinforces your attention to detail and ensures shared understanding from the start.

- *Why It Matters*: A written offer transforms conversation into commitment. It verifies that every negotiated term: salary, benefits, start date, and responsibilities, is clearly documented and mutually understood. This record protects both you and the employer, reducing the risk of confusion once you begin.

Addressing Counteroffers Respectfully

Topic: Evaluating a counteroffer from your current employer alongside a new opportunity.

- *What to Do:* Step back from the compensation details and compare the bigger picture: career trajectory, team culture, leadership style, and opportunity for growth. Look for patterns that show where you'll be challenged to expand your skills and trusted to take ownership. Choose the environment that reinforces progress through collaboration, respect, and consistent opportunities to contribute at a higher level.

- *Why It Matters*: Counteroffers often address compensation but rarely change the conditions that led you to explore new opportunities. Evaluating both roles through growth, culture, and leadership helps you see which one best supports your direction. An informed decision made on that basis strengthens your long-term credibility and reinforces the standard you set for how you approach each opportunity.

Discussing Career Development Opportunities

Topic: Exploring how the role supports your professional development and long-term growth.

- *What to Do*: Share that continued growth is important to you and ask how the company supports that development once the role officially starts. Listening to how they describe learning opportunities gives you a more realistic picture of whether growth is built into their culture or expected to happen independently.

- *Why It Matters*: How a company approaches professional development tells you how it manages potential. If growth is supported with established learning frameworks, the organization likely invests in long-term development. When it's left undefined, it may suggest that independent effort is valued but not consistently supported; an important distinction when choosing where to build your career.

Toolkit 6: Thank-You Email Toolkit

Introduction: Writing a thank-you email is one of the simplest ways to leave a positive impression after an interview. This toolkit helps you create a message that feels professional yet personal, reinforcing what you bring to the table while showing genuine appreciation for the opportunity. Each section offers flexible sentence options you can adapt to reflect your own tone, experience, and interest in the role.

Before You Begin

Send your thank-you email within one to two days of your interview, while the conversation is still fresh for both you and the interviewer. Keep your message short and focused on appreciation. The goal isn't to restate your conversation; it's to show that you listened, appreciated the discussion, and remain interested in the opportunity.

Start with a Thank You: Begin by expressing appreciation for the interviewer's time and the opportunity to learn more about the role. This sets a positive tone and reminds the reader that you value the conversation. Here are some easy options to get you started:

- *"Thank you for the opportunity to discuss the [Job Title] role at [Company Name]. I really appreciated learning more about your team."*

- *"Thank you for taking the time to meet with me to discuss the [Job Title] position at [Company Name]."*

- *"I appreciated the chance to learn more about the [Job Title] role and the priorities your team is focused on."*

- *"Thank you for taking the time to explain more about the [Job Title] position and how it contributes to [Company Name]'s goals."*

- *"I appreciated the opportunity to speak with you about the [Job Title] role and gain a better understanding of your team's approach."*

Show Your Interest: Your enthusiasm carries greater impact when it's tied to understanding. Referencing a key takeaway from the conversation shows that your excitement stems from awareness; of the role's impact, the team's goals, or the company's mission. Select one:

- *"Speaking with you gave me greater insight into the role and deepened my excitement about contributing to [specific goal/project] at [Company Name]."*

- *"Learning how the [Job Title] position supports [specific goal, initiative, or value] reinforced my enthusiasm about the opportunity."*

- *"Our discussion helped me see how my background could contribute meaningfully to [specific team, project, or company initiative]."*

- *"Understanding the goals of your team gave me a clearer picture of how I could contribute to your upcoming projects."*

- *"Hearing about [specific project or value] strengthened my interest in the work being done at [Company Name]."*

Highlight Your Fit and Key Qualifications: Mentioning something specific from your interview: like a project, goal, or idea discussed, shows you were fully engaged in the conversation and helps the interviewer remember your time together. Select one of the examples below that best fits your experience:

- *"The experience I bring in [relevant skill or focus area] aligns well with the objectives we discussed for the [Job Title] position."*

- *"My background in [relevant area] and ability to [specific skill or outcome] align closely with your team's goals."*

- *"The conversation confirmed how my experience in [specific skill or area] supports the work being done at [Company Name]."*

- *"Talking through [specific goal or responsibility] made it clear how my experience aligns with your team's needs."*

- *"I believe my experience in [specific focus area] connects well with the priorities you outlined for this role."*

Add a Personal Connection from Your Conversation: Mentioning something specific from your interview: like a project, goal, or idea discussed, shows you were fully engaged in the conversation and helps the interviewer remember your time together. Select one of the examples below to include in your message:

- *"I enjoyed hearing about [specific topic or project]; it gave me a real sense of how [Company Name] approaches its goals."*

- *"Learning more about [specific project, initiative, or unique aspect of the company] strengthened my appreciation for [Company Name]'s approach."*

- *"The discussion about [specific project or goal] resonated with me; it showed how closely my values align with [Company Name]'s mission."*

- *"Hearing about [specific topic or value] reinforced how well my professional approach aligns with your team's culture."*

- *"I appreciated your perspective on [specific company initiative or value]; it offered real insight into [Company Name]'s focus."*

Close by Sharing Your Enthusiasm for What's Ahead: End with a sentence that expresses appreciation while reinforcing your interest in continuing the conversation. This shows you value both the opportunity and the connection that began in the interview. Select one of the examples below to close your message:

- *"Thank you again for your time and consideration; I look forward to staying in touch."*

- *"I appreciate the opportunity to connect and discuss how I can contribute to your team's success."*

- *"Thanks again for taking the time to meet; please don't hesitate to reach out if I can provide any additional information."*

- *"I appreciated the opportunity to discuss the role and look forward to hearing about next steps."*

- *"Thank you again for the discussion; I hope to have the opportunity to continue the conversation."*

Final Step: Close your email with a simple, professional sign-off such as:

- "Best regards,"

- "Kind regards,"

- "Sincerely,"

and then add your name.

Example Emails Using the Toolkit

Here are two sample emails created using phrases from the toolkit:

Sample 1: *"Thank you for taking the time to meet with me to discuss the [Job Title] position at [Company Name]. Learning how the [Job Title] position supports [specific goal, initiative, or value] reinforced my enthusiasm about the opportunity. The experience I bring in [relevant skill or focus area] aligns well with the objectives we discussed for the [Job Title] position. Thank you again for your time and consideration; I look forward to staying in touch."*
Best regards,
[Your Name]

Sample 2: *"It was helpful to talk through the [Job Title] responsibilities and understand how the position supports [Company Name]. I'd value any insight you're able to provide about my interview performance or how I presented my experience. I know your schedule is busy, and I'm grateful for any time you can dedicate to sharing feedback. I value the conversation we had and hope our paths cross again in the future."*
Kind regards,
[Your Name]

Making It Your Own

You now have every piece needed to write a thank-you email that feels personal, respectful, and professional. Think of these examples as starting points; meant to help you structure your message, not replace your voice.

A professional thank-you note does more than express appreciation; it confirms your interest, reinforces your professionalism, and leaves a deeper understanding of how you think and communicate. Use this opportunity to show that your professionalism extends beyond the interview, into every part of your communication.

Toolkit 7: Feedback Request Email Toolkit

Introduction: This toolkit helps you request feedback after an interview in a way that encourages reflection and learning. Asking for feedback is a professional habit that shows maturity, humility, and a desire to grow. Whether you were selected for the role or not, this step can turn each interview into a valuable learning experience. Use one phrase from each section to create a personalized message that reflects your tone, reinforces professionalism, and encourages honest, helpful feedback.

Before You Begin

Before reaching out, confirm that the interview process has finished or that a decision has been communicated. The goal of this request is to learn from the experience, not to revisit the result. Waiting to send it at the right time reinforces that you understand professional boundaries and that your interest in feedback comes from reflection rather than expectation.

Opening Line – Reconnecting Professionally: Begin with a professional greeting that references your recent interview and keeps the focus on connection rather than appreciation. For example, you might start by referencing your earlier conversation rather than the opportunity itself. Select one of the sample statements below to begin your message.

- *"I wanted to thank you for taking the time to meet with me regarding the [Job Title] position at [Company Name]."*

- *"It was great speaking with you about the [Job Title] position and learning more about your team's approach at [Company Name]."*

- *"I appreciated the opportunity to discuss the [Job Title] position and learn how the role contributes to [Company Name]'s goals."*

- *"It was helpful to talk through the [Job Title] responsibilities and understand how the position supports [Company Name]."*

- *"Thank you again for the conversation about the [Job Title] role; I enjoyed learning more about your team and the work being done at [Company Name]."*

Expressing Interest in Feedback: Your request for feedback communicates that you value continuous learning and skill development. It shows you're willing to take responsibility for your growth and see each interview as an opportunity to improve. The key is to ask in a way that reflects curiosity about how you presented yourself. Select one of the examples below that best fits your tone and purpose:

- *"If possible, I'd appreciate any feedback you can share that could help me strengthen my interview approach."*

- *"I'd value any insight you're able to provide about my interview performance or how I presented my experience."*

- *"If there are areas you think I could improve for future opportunities, I'd be grateful for your perspective."*

- *"I'm always looking to learn from each experience, so any observations you can share would be appreciated."*

- *"I'd appreciate any feedback you're comfortable sharing that could help me continue developing my professional skills."*

Acknowledging Time and Effort: Acknowledging the interviewer's time shows that you value their effort as much as the opportunity to learn from the process. Taking a moment to thank them for their perspective shows maturity and helps strengthen future professional connections. Select one of the examples below to include in your message.

- *"I understand that sharing feedback takes time, and I appreciate your willingness to do so."*

- *"I know your schedule is busy, and I'm grateful for any time you can dedicate to sharing feedback."*

- *"I appreciate the time and consideration involved in providing feedback."*

- *"Thank you for taking the time to share your perspective; it's truly appreciated."*

- *"I understand that providing feedback requires additional effort, and I value the insight you're able to offer."*

Closing Line – Staying Positive and Open to Future Opportunities: Your closing line shows how you approach closure; an often-overlooked part of professional communication. It reinforces that you can bring an interaction to a close with respect, composure, and awareness, leaving others with a clear sense of your professionalism. Select one of the closing statements below to include in your message.

- *"Thank you again for your time; I hope we can stay in touch."*

- *"I appreciate your time throughout this process and wish continued success to you and your team."*

- *"Thank you for considering my request; I look forward to staying connected."*

- *"I value the conversation we had and hope our paths cross again in the future."*

- *"I appreciate your time and feedback; I wish you and your team continued success."*

Final Step: Close your email with a professional sign-off that reflects the tone of your message:

- "Best regards,"

- "Kind regards,"

- "Sincerely,"

and then add your name.

Example Emails Using the Toolkit

Here are two sample emails created using phrases from the toolkit:

Sample 1: *"I wanted to thank you for taking the time to meet with me regarding the [Job Title] position at [Company Name]. If possible, I'd appreciate any feedback you can share that could help me strengthen my interview approach. I understand that sharing feedback takes time, and I appreciate your willingness to do so. Thank you for considering my request; I look forward to staying connected."*
Best regards,
[Your Name]

Sample 2: *"It was helpful to talk through the [Job Title] responsibilities and understand how the position supports [Company Name]. I'd value any insight you're able to provide about my interview performance or how I presented my experience. I know your schedule is busy, and I'm grateful for any time you can dedicate to sharing feedback. I value the conversation we had and hope our paths cross again in the future."*
Kind regards,
[Your Name]

Making It Your Own

You now have every piece needed to request feedback in a way that shows reflection, self-awareness, and respect for the process. These examples are here to help you organize your thoughts, but your tone and intent should align with how you naturally communicate in professional settings.

A strong feedback request isn't about asking for approval; it's about showing that you value professional growth and understand the importance of continued learning. Each message you send shows that you approach communication with maturity and are comfortable seeking insight that helps you progress.

Toolkit 8: Networking Strategy Workshop

Introduction: Building a network doesn't start with luck; it starts with intention. A strong network supports more than your next opportunity: it strengthens your understanding of your field, connects you to new perspectives, and often leads to unexpected collaborations. The goal isn't to treat networking as a numbers game, but to create professional relationships built on respect, curiosity, and shared value.

Step 1: Define Your Networking Goals: Identify what you want to accomplish from your networking efforts. Are you exploring new roles, seeking mentorship, learning about emerging trends, or looking to build a professional support system.

- *What to Do*: Write down two or three specific goals that feel both achievable and meaningful to you. Under each, list the types of people who could help you take the next step: professionals in roles you aspire to, mentors who can offer guidance, or peers who share similar interests. Include what you can contribute to those relationships, whether that's knowledge, encouragement, or collaboration. Treat this list as a living document; you can refine it as your priorities shift.

- *Why It Matters*: Having a focused goal shifts networking from a series of random interactions into an intentional conversation. When you know what you're focused on, each connection feels natural rather than forced. This awareness helps you recognize where to invest your time and energy; creating relationships that support both your current direction and the decisions that support your long-term professional goals.

Step 2: Identify Key Contacts: Identify who can help you take the next step toward your professional goals. These may include past colleagues, mentors, alumni, community members, or professionals whose work you respect. Understanding who fits where in your network helps you focus your time where it has the most impact.

- *What to Do*: Create a list of people who support your goals and recognize what makes each connection valuable; write down their name, role, organization, and how you're connected. Add notes about shared experiences, professional interests, or mutual contacts that could strengthen how you connect with each contact. If someone feels slightly outside your immediate circle but connects with your direction, include them as a potential connection to develop over time. Return to this list when making career decisions to see which connections can offer insight or direction.

- *Why It Matters*: Identifying who can contribute to your progress helps you approach networking with a clear plan for who to connect with and why. It allows you to see where real opportunities exist; who offers perspective, who provides access, and who helps you think through key decisions. Over time, this awareness becomes a professional advantage. You'll know where to invest your time, who to stay in touch with, and when to seek input before taking action.

Step 3: Outreach Strategies: Learn to connect with others through communication that reflects interest, professionalism, and respect; effective outreach isn't about who you know, it's about how you engage.

- *What to Do:* Create a list of contacts you'd like to reach out to, then draft a personalized message for each one. Mention something specific about their work or shared interests that shows you've taken time to learn about them. Keep your tone professional yet conversational, and let them know what part of their background or experience drew your interest. For example, you might say, *"I'd appreciate hearing how you approached your transition into project management"* or *"I'd love your perspective on how the field is evolving for early-career professionals."* Decide when to follow up if you don't receive a reply; planning ahead turns waiting into part of your strategy, not a setback *(about a week is usually appropriate).*

- *Why It Matters:* How you reach out often determines whether someone chooses to engage. Each correspondence reflects the standards you bring to your work; whether you pay attention to details, take initiative, or leave communication open-ended. Consistency in how you approach people builds quiet credibility; the kind that shows people your professionalism extends beyond titles or roles.

Email Template for Reaching Out to a New Contact

Subject: Connecting on [Topic or Area of Interest] – [Your Name]

Dear [Contact's Name],

I recently saw your profile on [mention platform or connection] and was impressed by [mention something specific about their background or work]. As I am currently [briefly describe your professional status], I'd love to connect and hear more about your experience in [mention any specific area of interest].

Would you be open to sharing any insights on [mention specific topic]? If you're available, I'd love to schedule a short call. I'm free at [provide two time options] and can adjust based on your availability.

Thank you in advance for your time, and I hope we have a chance to connect!

Kind regards,

[Your Name]

[Your LinkedIn profile link or professional website]

Step 4: Engage Regularly: Maintain awareness of what's happening across your professional network. Regular engagement keeps you connected to transitions, projects, and collaborations that relate back to your goals.

- *What to Do:* Create a simple plan to stay in touch with people in your network throughout the year. Reach out when you have a reason that supports the connection; to share new insights, follow up on a past discussion, or acknowledge someone's professional milestone. Be intentional about the content and timing of your messages so each interaction feels purposeful rather than habitual, reinforcing trust, maintaining visibility, and strengthening the professional connection over time.

- *Why It Matters*: Consistent, purposeful engagement ensures you stay aware of developments in your network, such as new projects, role changes, or collaborations. It keeps your name present in conversations where opportunities arise, increasing the likelihood that you are considered for roles, advice, or introductions. By connecting new interactions to what was discussed earlier, you reinforce the relevance of the relationship and its potential for collaboration. This approach strengthens connections that can actively support your career growth while creating a network that remains relevant, responsive, and mutually beneficial.

Step 5: Leverage Social Media: Your online presence is an extension of your professional identity. Using social platforms strategically allows you to stay informed, build credibility, and ensure the people who can open doors, provide guidance, or collaborate with you understand the value you bring.

- *What to Do:* Keep your social media profiles updated with your latest experiences, skills, and achievements relevant to your area of expertise. Schedule consistent, intentional engagement: comment on a colleague's post to share insight or encouragement, participate in discussions about industry trends, or share articles paired with a short reflection on how they relate to your work. Reference past conversations or shared interests where appropriate to make interactions relevant. Even brief, consistent actions like acknowledging milestones, highlighting trends, or contributing a perspective help you stay visible, share expertise, and show that you follow developments in your field while staying connected to key people.

- *Why It Matters*: Social media is a window into the conversations, trends, and developments that impact your field. By engaging in regular interaction, referencing prior discussions, and sharing relevant insights, you ensure your contributions are noticed by the right people. This presence reinforces the value of your professional relationships and keeps you aware of the conversations impacting your field.

Step 6: Evaluate and Adapt: Your professional network holds insights into both opportunities and gaps in your strategy. Taking a look at your engagement helps you see where relationships have led to results and where a different approach could lead to better outcomes.

- *What to Do:* Set aside time at regular intervals to review your networking efforts. Look at the results of your interactions; new contacts, advice received, introductions, or opportunities that were identified. Identify which strategies produced the most valuable responses and which connections or approaches could benefit from a few minor adjustments. Capture insights about your own engagement style and how others respond to it; these discoveries can guide how you build stronger, more authentic relationships. Use this understanding to focus on methods that strengthen key connections, deepen engagement, and create opportunities that align with your goals and professional growth.

- *Why It Matters*: Evaluating your networking helps you see which interactions led to valuable advice, introductions, or opportunities, and which efforts didn't have the desired impact. By capturing insights about how others respond and adjusting your approach, you can build relationships that feel authentic, maintain trust, and position you as someone who builds strong professional relationships. Over time, this intentional reflection helps you balance your own goals with the needs and growth of your network.

Final Thoughts

The way you build relationships says a lot about how you approach growth;
your network becomes both a reflection and a resource. Look for patterns
in your interactions: which conversations create insight, provide guidance,
or open doors? Write down small takeaways from each interaction and apply one insight from each to improve how you connect with others. Over
time, these reflections help you focus on the connections that truly matter,
strengthen trust, and create opportunities that benefit both you and the people in your network. Networking becomes not just a professional task, but a
practice of learning, adapting, and growing alongside others.

Toolkit 9: Digital Footprint Workshop

Introduction: Your digital footprint often makes the first impression long before you do. This toolkit helps you assess how your online presence reflects your character, values, and goals: because what appears about you online often influences how others choose to engage with you. By reviewing and refining what's visible, you take greater control of how your professional story is understood, keeping it aligned with your current goals.

Step 1: Google Yourself

- ***What to Do***: Search your name in multiple search engines and review what appears on the first few pages. Try a few variations, such as including your city, school, or current company (for example, *"Alex R. Smith San Diego"* or *"Alex Smith Project Coordinator"*). Look for social media profiles, photos, or mentions connected to your name, and write down anything that stands out. Ask yourself whether each result represents who you are today or reflects an earlier stage in your life or career. Understanding how your information appears publicly allows you to make relevant updates, reinforce the image you want to project, and identify areas that may need more context or improvement.

- ***Why It Matters***: The internet never forgets, but you can manage what it remembers. In today's world, your online footprint can be just as important as your resume. Ensuring that your public footprint is up to date and professional sets you up for credible first impressions with potential employers, clients, and colleagues who are likely to search for you online before meeting you.

Step 2: Social Media Profiles Audit

- *What to Do*: Review every social media account you've created: both active and inactive. Begin with the basics: your profile photo, headline, bio, and visible highlights. Ask whether these details accurately reflect your current professional direction. Check that employment dates, roles, and contact information are current. Archive or update anything that no longer fits who you are today, such as outdated achievements or casual language in public bios. Adjust privacy settings to ensure personal content remains within your comfort zone and that professional details stay consistent with your experience, values, and intended direction.

- *Why It Matters*: Your profiles influence how others decide whether to reach out, collaborate, or consider you for opportunities. Think of social media as your virtual business card; it's often the first introduction to your professional reputation and values. Profiles that reflect your current work suggest that you stay engaged with your field. When details are accurate, they make it easier for others to connect your experience with current needs in your field.

Step 3: Professional Content Review

- *What to Do*: Review your recent posts, comments, and shared content with an awareness of what they communicate about your judgment and communication style. Look for examples where tone, language, or reaction could be interpreted differently than intended. Consider how you engage with others: whether you add value, offer insight, or distract from the purpose of the conversation. Write down any examples that might weaken your credibility, and replace them with contributions that reflect balance, respect, and awareness of your role in the conversation.

- *Why It Matters:* Every post or comment becomes part of your professional reputation. The way you respond to others shows how you manage differing opinions and whether you can engage without losing perspective. Consistent, measured communication builds credibility, helping others view you as someone whose input carries weight and whose presence adds value to the conversation.

Step 4: LinkedIn Specifics

- *What to Do:* Create a headline that highlights your professional direction rather than just your title. For example, instead of "Marketing Assistant," you could write "Marketing Assistant | Focused on Digital Strategy and Brand Growth." Use this space to show where your interests and strengths meet. Review your profile for consistency with your professional background, including recent work, academic projects, or volunteer experiences that reflect growth. Request recommendations from people who can speak to how you work, not just what you've done. Stay active by commenting on, sharing, or posting content that reflects interest in your field, helping others see you as engaged and informed.

- *Why It Matters:* LinkedIn extends your professional reputation beyond your résumé. Employers and peers often use it to confirm how you present yourself, who you engage with, and what you contribute to your field. A consistently maintained profile builds credibility before introductions happen, reinforcing your credibility in ways that make future conversations more productive.

Step 5: Strengthen Your Professional Brand

- *What to Do:* Use your online presence to reinforce the professional direction you want to be known for. On platforms like LinkedIn, X (formerly Twitter), or Instagram, share insights, updates, or reflections that connect to your field, your growth, or the values driving your professional approach. On more creative or visual platforms, such as TikTok or YouTube, consider sharing short observations, helpful insights, or project updates that reflect your curiosity and initiative. Include personal elements: volunteer work, community involvement, or hobbies that show commitment or learning to add dimension to your profile. Work toward consistency in tone across platforms so your online activity reinforces your professional reputation.

- *Why It Matters:* Your professional brand influences how easily others can understand what you offer. When your public interactions online reflect the same professionalism you bring to your work, it helps people recognize how you operate before they meet you. That consistency shortens the distance between introduction and opportunity, because others can see proof of the way you conduct yourself through what you share.

Step 6: Monitor Regularly

- *What to Do:* Review your digital footprint on a monthly basis to ensure it aligns with your current goals. Update LinkedIn, social media, or your personal website with recent projects, achievements, or experiences that reflect your current direction. Review your photo and bio for relevance to your goals and adjust if needed. Set up tools like Google Alerts for your name so you're notified when new information appears about you. Treat this as routine maintenance: a proactive habit that keeps you prepared for new opportunities by ensuring what others find about you remains accurate.

- *Why It Matters:* Your digital footprint continues to evolve, even when you're not actively updating it. Regular monitoring keeps you aware of what others can see and how that information might shape their first impression. By staying informed and making small updates over time, you prevent outdated or incomplete details from creating confusion about your experience or direction. Taking ownership of this process ensures your professional reputation stays focused on where you're headed, not where you've been.

Step 7: Optimize for Visibility

- ***What to Do:*** Make your online profiles easier for the right people to find. Review the language you use in your LinkedIn headline, summary, and experience sections to ensure it includes terms that reflect your skills and goals. Think about how someone searching for your background would describe it, then include those same words in your profile. For instance, if you work in marketing, keywords like *"content strategy," "brand development,"* or *"campaign analytics"* can help potential employers recognize your value quickly. Update your skills section with terms that match your experience and review job postings for your preferred roles to identify which words appear most often. The goal is quiet consistency: so what appears online reflects where your focus is today.

- ***Why It Matters:*** Visibility is more than being seen; it's about being understood. The words you choose influence the way others interpret your experience, helping potential employers or collaborators connect your background with their needs. When your profile reflects both what you've done and where you're heading, it creates alignment between your capabilities and the opportunities most relevant to you. This understanding strengthens your professional presence, helping others recognize your fit before a conversation even begins.

Make It Your Own

You now have a structured way to refine your digital presence; this process is personal. How you manage what's visible online reflects self-awareness, judgment, and an understanding of professional perception. It's less about meeting expectations and more about aligning visibility with authenticity. These questions help you examine the connection between what others see and what you want them to take away.

- *When someone searches for you online, what do you want them to understand about you before you meet?*

- *Are there parts of your professional story that aren't yet visible but should be; such as volunteer work, certifications, or personal projects?*

- *Do your current posts, photos, or comments reflect the direction you want your career to take?*

- *How often do you review your online presence to ensure it reflects your growth and priorities?*

- *What small updates; like a refined headline, concise bio, or updated keywords; could help position you for future opportunities?*

Toolkit 10: Career Fair Strategies

Introduction: Many people walk into career fairs hoping to stand out. The real advantage comes from walking in prepared to *learn*. Every booth, conversation, and brief exchange offers insight into what companies value and how they make decisions. How you approach the event; from preparation to follow-up, influences what you learn and how you grow from the experience; whether that's discovering new interests, building connections, or gaining perspective on how employers connect individual strengths with organizational needs. Seen through this lens, career fairs become less about outcomes and more about alignment; between who you are and where you want to go.

Preparation Strategies

Research Companies: Start by identifying the organizations that you find worth learning more about; not just the ones with familiar names. Review their company pages, recent announcements, and job descriptions to understand what kind of work they prioritize and how they talk about it. Look for patterns in the language they use, the values they emphasize, and the skills they highlight.

Look at where the company is investing time, talent, or funding to understand its trajectory: *Are they expanding into new markets? Investing in innovation? Strengthening community partnerships?* These insights help you evaluate fit; not just opportunity; before starting a conversation.

When you arrive at the career fair, this preparation allows you to engage recruiters with informed curiosity. It shows you've invested time to understand their world; and helps you identify which environments would make the best use of your strengths.

Preparation Strategies

Your Pitch: How you introduce yourself says a lot about how you understand your own value. A strong pitch connects how you work, what you've learned, and why it deserves attention. The Personal Pitch Workshop from Toolkit #1 gives you a place to begin; refining your message helps you show how your experience connects to an organization's priorities in a way that reflects your approach, not just your responsibilities.

When developing your pitch, describe the steps you took: what you faced, what you decided needed attention, and what changed because of your actions. The situations don't need to be impressive; they need to show the reasoning behind what you did: how you noticed what needed improvement, chose a direction, and made it work better. This might involve resolving a recurring issue, or responding to change with reasoning rather than reaction.

If your experience comes from school, volunteering, or another field, you can describe what carried over: the awareness that helps you see connections others might miss, the adaptability that supports steady adjustment, and the curiosity that strengthens how you learn from experience. Practicing your pitch also helps you understand how your examples come across when someone else is listening; you'll notice whether they make sense without extra explanation or rely on what you assume others already know.

Preparation Strategies

Get Your Resume Ready: Your resume reflects how you understand the relevance of your work: how you organize it, interpret it, and present it for someone else to evaluate. Review it as if you were seeing it for the first time; each section should tell the reader what you know, how you've applied it, and where it led. Remove details that no longer represent your direction and expand on those that do.

If you're meeting several employers, adjust your resume slightly for each one. Each version should reflect what you've learned about their work; what they build, manage, or improve. Small adjustments in how you sequence or describe results help communicate awareness: that you understand not only what you've done but how it relates to the environments you want to join.

How you prepare your resume reflects how you think through interactions. Each choice; the order of sections, the choice of words, the consistency in presentation; shows how you translate personal experience into information someone else can use. The document becomes a small example of how you manage responsibility: reading context, anticipating needs, and communicating in a way that supports another person's decision.

Preparation Strategies

Look the Part: Professional appearance is less about formality than awareness. At a career fair, what you wear and how you carry yourself show that you understand the expectations of the environment and the kind of attention you hope to earn. Dress in a way that supports how you want to be remembered; it should help others focus on the impression your words create, not compete with it.

Your presentation communicates more than composure; it shows how you think about preparation when the outcome depends on perception. The fit and condition of your clothing show how you manage the small details that play a role in early impressions. These details tell others whether you're organized, aware of expectations, and consistent in your work. They're not about fashion or style; they're about awareness. When you connect presentation with purpose, you show that you understand what the environment asks of you and that you're capable of adapting without losing authenticity.

Professional presence extends beyond clothing. How you stand, move, and listen affects how others experience the interaction. The way you stay connected to the conversation shows that you're prepared to participate rather than perform. These quiet forms of awareness support dialogue that develops naturally and help others stay engaged with what you're saying rather than how you appear.

At the Event

Map Out Your Visits: A career fair is one of the few settings where employers expect you to ask questions and think out loud about your direction. Each discussion helps you hear how organizations describe their work, what they emphasize, and where your skills have the greatest impact.

When planning your strategy, think in terms of perspective rather than proximity. Begin with organizations that align with your experience, then add a few that test what you think you know about your field. Include employers whose work relates to your interests in direct and indirect ways; the first keeps you grounded, the second broadens your view. Hearing how organizations explain what drives their work can make it easier to recognize which roles connect with your interests.

Once the fair begins, rely on your preparation to start conversations, then notice how each conversation feels; some inform, some connect. Pay attention to the pattern of dialogue; where engagement builds, where energy fades, and where conversation turns into a real exchange of ideas. Those observations can help you decide when to wait, when to approach, and when to move on. The value you take away comes not from how many people you meet but from recognizing which conversations offered insight into what you're drawn to; and why.

At the Event

Engage Effectively: Engagement begins with awareness: knowing when to speak, when to listen, and when to let curiosity guide the next question. Each conversation is both information and interpretation; it reflects how you take in what's being said and how you respond. Use your pitch as an entry point, then let it develop into dialogue.

When you approach a booth, pause long enough to understand the dynamic. Notice how representatives engage: the questions they ask and the points they return to. These cues help you enter the conversation with awareness rather than hesitation. Once engaged, focus on what they consider important: connect your experience to what they've emphasized and ask questions that clarify what they look for in a candidate. Pay attention to how they respond. When someone expands on a topic or redirects the discussion, it often indicates what they view as most important. The value comes from responding to what you hear, not rehearsing what you planned to say.

Before you move on, summarize key points from your discussion or confirm next steps if they've been mentioned. Close with appreciation that feels professional, not practiced. Confirming mutual understanding shows that you were attentive to the discussion and respectful of their time. Every conversation reveals how professionalism is less about what you present and more about how you interpret what's given back.

At the Event

Take Notes: Most people leave a conversation remembering how it felt, not what was learned. It's when you can still hear the recruiter's phrasing, sense the tone, and recall what captured their interest, before those details fade into general impressions. Capturing these moments turns observation into understanding; helping you identify what prompted follow-up questions or topic changes.

Your notes show what actually happened: what was said, what mattered, and what changed once the conversation began. Look for points that required adjustment: a question that challenged your assumptions, a comment that shifted the topic, or feedback that caught you off guard. Include small reminders, such as a recruiter's preferred contact method.

This process builds a form of applied intelligence. By reviewing factual detail instead of impressions, you begin linking cause and effect; how phrasing influenced reaction, how timing affected tone, how structure framed response. It helps you replace interpretation with insight, so what you learn becomes something you can apply. Structured notes turn a day of conversations into usable data: who to contact, when to follow up, and what to reference in your next message. Remember, the value of your notes isn't in what they capture, but in what they help you recognize.

Post-Event Follow-Up

- *Send Thank-You Notes*: Follow up within one business day while the discussion is still fresh for both of you. Reference a specific point from your conversation: a topic, initiative, or perspective that made the exchange stand out. A well-written follow-up proves you listened; you understood what was said, acted on it, and closed the loop. That level of response turns conversation into credibility.

- *Connect on LinkedIn*: Reach out within a few days of the event with a short, specific message. Mention where you met and include one memorable point from your discussion: something that reflects real interest in their work or awareness of their perspective. Reaching out this way shows you value the discussion, not just the contact. It keeps the connection professional and easy to build on later.

- *Track Your Applications*: Keep a short record of each application and track what happened after: who responded, how quickly, and what kind of message earned their attention. Those notes help you see the connection between what you communicated and how it was received; turning response patterns into professional insight. When you review them, you'll start to see trends in how your communication performs across roles and industries. That awareness helps you adjust naturally; you start to see what connects, what doesn't, and why.

Toolkit 11: Interview Curveballs

Introduction: Some interview questions are designed to test what can't be rehearsed; your mindset, adaptability, and comfort with uncertainty. This toolkit helps you turn those unpredictable moments into your advantage. Each exercise is meant to strengthen the mindset interviewers value most: composed, structured reasoning when the unexpected happens.

Strategies for Response: Strategies for Response: When planning your responses, focus on staying calm and thinking logically. Avoid rushing to fill the silence. Stay focused on expressing your reasoning step-by-step rather than jumping to conclusions. This demonstrates emotional control, critical thinking, and the presence of mind to handle unplanned situations effectively. Remember, the goal isn't to have a perfect answer but to show how you think.

Examples of Potential Surprise Questions

"If you were an animal, what would you be and why?"

- *Purpose*: Tests creativity and self-perception.

- *What to Do*: Select an animal that best represents qualities you be-lieve are important for the role. For example, in a leadership posi-tion, choosing a lion could show your confidence and decision-mak-ing strength. Or, if applying for a collaborative role, you might choose a dolphin for its teamwork and intelligence. Before the inter-view, think about traits you value in yourself, such as adaptability, self-awareness, or empathy, and how those could connect to the position. Doing this before the interview lets you describe the con-nection between personal traits and professional impact.

- *Why It Matters*: This question invites you to connect self-awareness with your approach to professional situations. The way you explain your answer shows whether you understand what the role requires and how your qualities fit within that context. It's less about the animal itself and more about how clearly you can link traits to pro-fessional behaviors.

"How many golf balls can fit in a school bus?"

- **Purpose**: Evaluates your problem-solving process and comfort with ambiguity.

- **What to Do**: Treat this as a test of reasoning, not accuracy. Begin by outlining your approach; estimate the dimensions of a standard school bus, then gauge how much space a golf ball would occupy. Explain your logic clearly as you calculate, acknowledging any assumptions along the way. You could also mention other variables you'd consider; like unused space, seats, or windows; to show that you're thinking realistically about constraints rather than making random guesses. Explaining how each estimate connects to your reasoning shows control of your process and confidence in the conclusions you reach.

- **Why It Matters**: This question shows how well you manage situations that don't have clear answers. Interviewers watch for your ability to stay composed, explain your reasoning, and make logical choices without overcomplicating the situation. These same skills translate to professional settings where information is incomplete, yet decisions still need to be made responsibly.

"If you could have dinner with anyone, living or dead, who would it be and why?"

- **Purpose**: Reflects values, interests, and personality.

- **What to Do**: Choose someone whose life or work aligns with qualities that you admire or strive to develop. This might be someone who expanded your thinking, inspired resilience, or exemplifies leadership in a way that connects to your goals. Explain not only who you chose, but why; what about their character, achievements, or mindset has influenced how you approach your own growth. For example, choosing a scientist, educator, or community leader could show your respect for innovation, learning, or service.

- **Why It Matters**: This question helps interviewers understand what drives your curiosity and what you value in others. The way you explain your choice reflects how you gain insight from the people who inspire you and your openness to learning from diverse perspectives. It also gives a view into how self-awareness influences what kind of teammate or leader you'll become.

"Sell me this pen."

- **Purpose**: Tests your ability to connect with others through clear communication and insight into their needs.

- **What to Do**: Approach this question as a conversation, not a sales pitch. Begin by asking questions to understand what the buyer values; do they care about quality, reliability, or presentation? Once you learn what matters most to them, connect the pen's features to their priorities. You might emphasize how it feels comfortable for long writing sessions; or how its modern design fits a professional setting. Showing curiosity about their needs before describing the product shows awareness, empathy, and the ability to stay composed.

- **Why It Matters**: This question lets you show that persuasion begins with understanding. By identifying what the buyer values before speaking, you reinforce awareness, active listening, and the discipline to think before you respond; skills that strengthen credibility in interviews and professional discussions alike.

"What would you do if you found out your best work friend was stealing?"

- **Purpose**: Evaluates ethical judgment, emotional maturity, and fairness in difficult situations.

- **What to Do**: Show that you value integrity without disregarding empathy. Start by explaining that you would take time to confirm the facts before reacting; acknowledging the seriousness of the issue while avoiding assumptions. Then describe how you would address the situation responsibly, perhaps by encouraging your colleague to correct the behavior or by reporting it through the proper channels if necessary. This approach demonstrates accountability, discretion, and composure in handling sensitive workplace matters.

- **Why It Matters**: Ethical situations test more than what you believe; they show how you apply those beliefs when personal connections are involved. Interviewers watch for signs that you can slow down, focus, and take actions that protect both people and principles. Showing that awareness reinforces that your decisions come from reflection, not reaction.

"Tell me something that's true, that almost nobody agrees with you on."

- **Purpose**: Evaluates independent thinking, depth of reasoning, and comfort with differing viewpoints.

- **What to Do**: Choose an opinion that reflects how you think about progress or improvement in your field, rather than something controversial or personal. Focus on ideas that show insight, curiosity, or a forward-thinking perspective. For example, you might say, *"I believe feedback should be ongoing instead of tied to annual reviews,"* and explain how this encourages better growth and accountability. What matters most is showing how you think through ideas that challenge convention, not whether others agree.

- **Why It Matters**: Preparing for questions like this helps you understand your own reasoning process: how you reach conclusions, explain them, and stay receptive to different views. That awareness improves how you communicate ideas, negotiate, and make decisions in your own career. The objective is to show that you can evaluate conflicting viewpoints through reasoning rather than reaction. The more you practice this kind of reflection, the stronger your ability becomes to lead discussions that bring people together rather than apart.

"What would you do if you were the CEO of our company for a day?"

- **Purpose**: Evaluates your understanding of the company, your ability to prioritize strategically, and how you think about leadership responsibility.

- **What to Do**: Treat this as a chance to show awareness, not authority. Begin by acknowledging that a single day isn't enough to make sweeping changes; but it is enough to observe, listen, and identify opportunities for impact. Choose one initiative tied to the company's goals or challenges. For example, if the company emphasizes innovation, you could suggest creating an open forum where employees share improvement ideas directly with leadership. Explain how your idea supports both the organization's mission and its people. Connect your answer to your own experience or perspective: for example, how taking time to listen and act on feedback strengthened relationships across the organization. This balance between strategic awareness and empathy reflects that you understand leadership as both directional and human.

- **Why It Matters**: This question helps interviewers understand how you think about influence, decision-making, and organizational health. The best responses show balance: considering vision, practicality, and how choices affect both results and relationships. Demonstrating awareness of company goals, paired with ideas that encourage engagement or efficiency, positions you as someone who views success from a broader, leadership-minded perspective.

Afterword

You've reached the end of *Interview Insights: A Strategic Approach*; yet the real work began when you started looking at the choices behind your own preparation. In that process, you evaluated how you organize your thinking, how you explain the reasoning behind your decisions, and how effectively you link your experience to what a listener needs to understand. You also recognized patterns in how you interpret questions and how those interpretations influence your responses. That distinction marks whether your response came from memory or from the steps you used to reach it.

This process can test anyone's confidence. You may have questioned whether your experience was enough, replayed moments you wish had gone differently, or wondered how to communicate what sets you apart without feeling scripted. Those doubts are part of learning to lead conversations rather than react to them. Each time you reframe an answer or study feedback, you strengthen the connection between what you know and how effectively you share it.

At The FLOW Series™ (https://theflowseries.com/), we've faced those same experiences firsthand; the mix of anticipation and uncertainty before interviews, the disconnect between what's asked and what feels expected, the small adjustments that strengthen how you present your reasoning. This book was built to turn those experiences into applied insight built from real interviews, decisions, and outcomes: a way to bring structure to preparation and meaning to each conversation.

Keep this book nearby as a reference point for your ongoing development. The concepts you've worked through aren't meant to create automatic responses; they're meant to help you study how you think: the choices you make, the assumptions you hold, and the patterns that influence your responses. When you revisit these ideas, you're not repeating a lesson; you're testing your awareness against new situations and higher expectations. Each review gives you the opportunity to refine how you interpret questions, manage uncertainty, and evaluate the quality of your own reasoning. As this becomes familiar, you'll start to see the difference between answering a question and explaining how you reached the answer.

One of the most useful outcomes of this work is learning to evaluate your own reasoning without needing someone else to point out what should change. When you can see the structure behind your explanations, you don't need external feedback to make adjustments. That ability stays with you because it's built on what you can observe in your own thinking.

Now it's time to keep building on that; one decision, one conversation, one opportunity at a time.

With Gratitude,

The FLOW Series Team

Next in The FLOW Series

The upcoming title, *Problem-Solving Insights: A Strategic Approach*, continues the style of thinking you explored in these pages. If this book strengthened how you organize your thoughts before a conversation, the next one shows how to review what led to a problem, separate what you know to be true from what you assumed, and decide what needs to happen next. The structure remains the same: understand your thinking first; then act.

www.ingramcontent.com/pod-product-compliance
Lightning Source LLC
Chambersburg PA
CBHW070655130626
46555CB00006B/2883

9798992747911